How to Be a Successful
Online Student

How to Be a Successful Online Student

Sara Dulaney Gilbert

McGraw-Hill

New York • San Francisco • Washington, D.C. • Auckland • Bogotá
Caracas • Lisbon • London • Madrid • Mexico City • Milan
Montreal • New Delhi • San Juan • Singapore
Sydney • Tokyo • Toronto

This book was set in Sabon by North Market Street Graphics.
Printed and bound by R. R. Donnelley & Sons Company.

McGraw-Hill books are available at special quantity discounts
to use as premiums and sales promotions, or for use in corporate
training programs. For more information, please write to the
Director of Special Sales, Professional Publishing, McGraw-Hill,
Two Penn Plaza, New York, NY 10121-2298. Or contact your
local bookstore.

 This book is printed on recycled, acid-free paper containing
a minimum of 50% recycled, de-inked fiber.

To Anna Julie Cruz
for all her special online expertise—
thanks, Julie!

Contents

Foreword

As president of University of Maryland University College (UMUC), one of the world's leading virtual universities, it is a distinct pleasure for me to address prospective online students in *How to Be a Successful Online Student*. In this high-tech Information Age, Sara Dulaney Gilbert has managed to translate much of today's language and cyber-speak about online education into a personal and easy-to-understand style, a more experiential how-to, if you will.

Sara addresses important issues, such as the level of proficiency required to master online technologies; whether online education is suitable to particular learner needs; how to identify appropriate academic programs and shop around for the best online deliverer; and how to be a successful learner in a Web-based environment. Learners need to realize that they can—and should—be served by a university that offers more than only courses online; they deserve electronic access to services of the entire university—for example, online admissions, course registration, and library services as well.

In describing elements of this increasingly popular delivery method, Sara does us all—students and universities—a great service by making online education concrete and real. Too often, discussions about distance learning are very abstract; few really address what online delivery means for students. Instead, we hear in more general terms of the online phenomenon, the education industry, the wealth of corporate universities and dot-coms, and implications for workforce development and higher education.

Certainly, the growth of online education alone demonstrates its increasing importance to today's lifelong learners. At UMUC, online enrollments have doubled or tripled each year since 1994, when the university began offering courses electronically. We have already surpassed 40,000 online enrollments thus far this past year.

But again, what does that mean to an individual student? UMUC online students attest that their e-courses require them to interact more frequently with fellow students and their professors than traditional courses. No student in an online course can sit at the "back of the classroom." It certainly means that, with the right professor and appropriate support, an online student can expect a truly enriching educational experience.

Our experience here in Maryland, where many of our online students reside, demonstrates clearly that even though they have easy access to nearby institutions, students today appreciate the convenience of pursuing their education when and where it suits them through online education. *Distance education* is, in fact, a misnomer, because it is not really just about distance anymore.

Online education is about creating agile learners who can operate in both human and technological environments with equal comfort. In my view, the greatest contribution of online education may not be conquering time and distance, but educating people for a new century. The readers of this book should think about online education in those terms as well as in terms of whether this method of delivery will help them get their degrees more quickly.

Dr. Gerald A. Heeger

Acknowledgments

The author would first like to thank Dr. Gerald A. Heeger, president of University of Maryland University College, for his time and thought in adding the kind and helpful words in the foreword of this book. Having worked with Dr. Heeger during his service as dean of New York University's School of Continuing and Professional Studies, I know that he is too modest to boast of his present institution, which is not only one of the oldest and largest providers of distance education, but also one of the most respected: indeed, a solid site in the world of virtual education.

The rest of the book owes its value as a firsthand guidebook to the contributions of the scores of distance learning teachers, designers, and participants from schools, colleges, universities, and other providers of training and education around North America who responded with information and ideas to requests and questionnaires distributed widely (via cyberspace, of course) throughout their information and association networks. Those who responded with generous comments and suggestions include:

Sheila Greve, Bergen Community College, Paramus, New Jersey

Joyce Feucht-Havier, California State University, Northridge

Larry Hannah and Mike Adams, California State University, Sacramento

Dawn Fuller and Chris Curran, University of Cincinnati, Cincinnati, Ohio

Bob Norden, Colorado Community Colleges On Line

Stephanie Leichnam, University of Dallas Graduate School of Management, Dallas, Texas

Jon Spors, Danville Area Community College, Danville, Illinois

Cindy Foley, Durham College, Oshawa, Ontario, Canada

Andreas Schramm and Professor A. M. Abbott, Graduate School of Education, Hamline University, St. Paul, Minnesota

Jane Brunk Kost, Jefferson College, Hillsboro, Missouri

Carol Crane, Maricopa Community College, Phoenix, Arizona

Bobbie Rubin, College of Marin, San Rafael, California

Nicole Simmons and Kathleen Stinehart, Mary Baldwin College, Staunton, Virginia

Keith Decie, University of Michigan Business School, Ann Arbor, Michigan

Mike Gleason, Millsaps College, Jackson, Mississippi

Karen Coffey, Kara Gabrielli, Roscoe Hastings, and Cathy Smith, Monroe Community College, Rochester, New York

Marion Flomenhaft and Joe Kornoski, Center of Career Education and Life Planning, New York University School of Continuing and Professional Studies, New York, New York

Cheri Kiefer and Fred Hurst, Northern Arizona University, Flagstaff, Arizona

Gale Spak, New Jersey Institute of Technology, Newark, New Jersey

Charlotte Kushner, Okanagan University College, Vancouver, British Columbia, Canada

Sister Teresita Hinnegan, University of Pennsylvania School of Nursing, Philadelphia, Pennsylvania

Gary Miller, World Campus at Penn State University, State College, Pennsylvania

John Sperling, University of Phoenix Online, Phoenix, Arizona

Judy Smith, Phoenix University, Phoenix Arizona, and University of Maryland University College, College Park, Maryland

John R. Sneed, Portland Community College, Portland, Oregon

Stacy Maloney, St. Mary's University, San Antonio, Texas

Larry Aft and Anupa Chakravarti, Southern Polytechnic University, Marietta, Georgia

Shannon Orser, Thomas Jefferson University College of Health Professions, Philadelphia, Pennsylvania

Dawn Madden, Training Associates, Atlanta, Georgia

Lisa Holloway, Tulsa Community College, Tulsa, Oklahoma

Loree Miltich, Claudette Harper, Jason Bock, Dan Price, and Tim Mott, The Union Institute, Cincinnati, Ohio

William Draves, Learning Resource Network, Manhattan, Kansas

Kevin Iness, student at University of Maryland University College

Connie Gibbs, Vancouver Community College, Vancouver, British Columbia, Canada

Tom Wilkinson, Virginia Polytechnic Institute and State University, Blacksburg, Virginia

Amelia Maretka, Wharton County Junior College, Wharton, Texas

As well as students, faculty, and administrators at Brevard Community College, Cocoa, Florida; University of California Extension, Los Angeles; California State University, Sacramento; Colorado State University, Fort Collins, Colorado; University of Dallas, Dallas, Texas; Jefferson College, Hillsboro, Missouri; Jones International University, Arlington, Florida; Marist College Business School, Poughkeepsie, New York; Regents College, Albany, New York; Thomas Edison State College, Trenton, New Jersey; and Wittenberg University, Springfield, Ohio.

Information on other providers was gathered from a variety of sources, but the personal touch shared by these contributors has greatly enhanced the material collected in this book.

Defining the Subject

Online learning is the new buzzword in education today. It's become shorthand for what is actually part of a bigger picture—distance learning. For an idea of what we're talking about, here are a few definitions:

Definitions of distance education

Distance Education is defined as a planned teaching/learning experience that uses a wide spectrum of technologies to reach learners at a distance and is designed to encourage learner interaction and certification of learning.

University of Wisconsin—Extension,
Continuing Education Extension,
Madison, Wisconsin

Distance Learning (DL) is an instructional delivery system which connects learners with educational resources. DL provides educational access to learners not enrolled in educational institutions and can augment the learning opportunities of current students. The implementation of DL is a process which uses available resources and will evolve to incorporate emerging technologies.

The California Distance Learning Project (CDLP),
Sacramento, California

Distance Education is instructional delivery that does not constrain the student to be physically present in the same location as the instructor. Historically, Distance Education meant correspondence study. Today, audio, video, and computer technologies are more common delivery modes.

> *The Distance Learning Resource Network (DLRN),*
> *U.S. Department of Education, Washington, DC*

Distance education (or correspondence/home study) is the enrollment and study with an educational institution which provides lesson materials prepared in a sequential and logical order for study by students on their own. When each lesson is completed the student makes available, by fax, mail, or computer, the assigned work for correction, grading, comment, and subject matter guidance by qualified instructors. Corrected assignments are returned to the student, an exchange which provides a personalized student-teacher relationship.

> *The Distance Education and Training Council (DETC),*
> *North Andover, Massachusetts*

Distance education is not simply the addition of technology to instruction; instead, it uses technology to make possible new approaches to the teaching/learning process.

> *Pennsylvania State Department of Distance Education,*
> *Office of Distance Education,*
> *State College, Pennsylvania*

Distance Education: the process of extending learning, or delivering instructional resource-sharing opportunities, to locations away from a classroom, building or site, to another classroom, building or site, by using video, audio, computer, multimedia communications, or some combination of these with other traditional delivery methods.

> *The Instructional Telecommunications Council (ITC),*
> *Washington, DC*

At its most basic level, distance education takes place when a teacher and student(s) are separated by physical distance, and technology (i.e., voice, video, data, and print), often in concert with face-to-face communication, is used to bridge the instructional gap.

The Engineering Outreach staff at the
University of Idaho, Moscow, Idaho

However it is defined, this kind of learning has made such a big impact on the education scene that the definitions and discussions spin off into apparently endless theory—in addition to all the high-tech spinning that goes on as well. This book is designed to make some of that clear—but, even more important, to help you turn it to practical use. The more you understand about this new learning marketplace, the more likely you are to gain A-student status. The information in the pages that follow will help you find your way through the maze of modern learning pathways—and come out ahead!

Explanation of Symbols

**Voice of
Experience**

**By the
Numbers**

**In Other
Words**

**Picture
This**

Fast Facts

**Check it
Out**

Part 1

Do You Need This Book?

Chapter 1
Why You Need This Book

Of course you need this book . . . if you're not a virtual student yet, chances are you will be soon. It seems that almost everybody is studying online—for undergraduate or graduate degrees, as lifelong learning, or for professional or technical training—and we all want to achieve success.

But you may need this book for other reasons as well. The numbers of schools, programs, courses, and students engaged in distance learning are growing at an explosive rate—so rapidly that directories and listings can't come close to keeping up with the new offerings. In this high-growth environment, the buzz about distance learning rapidly turns to hype, and the hype is designed to pull you in—even into courses that aren't right for you. This is not a marketing fad or a fun-and-games activity: the right (or wrong) program can make a huge difference in your life. Fortunately, behind the hype are plenty of facts.

By the Numbers

The number of colleges offering online degrees doubled in a single year, according to a report from Market Data Retrieval, which surveyed some 4000 higher education institutions. In 1999–2000, 34 percent of two- and four-year colleges offered degrees via computer, compared to 15 percent the year before. In addition to full degrees, 7 in 10 colleges offer some sort of distance learning, including courses, lecture notes, and online study groups. Continuing the expansion, one-third of colleges surveyed also spent additional funds on technology and added computers to dorms and classrooms, up from just 25 percent the previous year. Furthermore, most other education providers—from corporate training programs to lifelong learning institutions—rely extensively on distance education, and multiple for-profit education providers are creating fierce competition for the online students and their tuition.

To help you focus on the facts, we begin the old-fashioned way—
with (what else?) a pop quiz.

First, pick the best phrase or phrases to finish this sentence:

An online student . . .

  (a) Can get a degree in pajamas without leaving the bedroom

  (b) Can save a lot of education time and money

  (c) Will have no interaction with actual classmates or professors

  (d) Has to be really computer-smart

  (e) All of the above

  (f) None of the above

Now, try this true/false question:

  1. Anyone can succeed as an online student.   T   F

  2. All distance education requires a computer.   T   F

  3. The best online programs are from the best-rated colleges.   T   F

  4. All distance programs give the same credentials as on-campus
     classes.   T   F

  5. People who have finished school won't ever need online learning.   T   F

Stumped? Maybe. More likely, even if you think you made a perfect
score, you'll probably be surprised by the answers you got wrong.
Even highly successful online students, no matter what their age,
background, or interest, say that before embarking on their project,
they had to clear away a cloud of misconceptions that interfered
with making practical decisions about their studies. Others, often
less successful, now say they wish they had had a clearer picture of
the distance education process ahead of time. It's true that distance
learning, especially the online variety, is part of a revolution in
learning (we go into that further in Chapter 2). Keep in mind that
until only a few years ago, even the idea of putting tuition on a
credit card was out of the question. Education has changed so fast

in so many ways (including its advertising) that we seem to have leaped from the nineteenth century straight into the twenty-first—so it's no wonder we expect miracles.

Success scorecard

However, as you'll learn in this book, success in online learning is still as dependent on some old-fashioned factors as it is on high-tech savvy. For example, you need to put as much effort into shopping for the right course as you would into taking on-campus tours or studying a paper catalog. True, the facts are available at your fingertips and come up on your computer screen, but they still require thorough research and careful judgment.

To start, review the answers to the quiz. For the multiple choice question, the answer is (f), *None of the above*. The other possible answers illustrate some of the prevalent misconceptions about distance learning. For example:

(a) *Can get a degree in pajamas without leaving the bedroom.* An online student might be able to earn a degree without leaving home in certain very limited cases, but programs designed to keep students off campus for their entire educational careers are few and rare. At the very least, you'll probably have to show up somewhere for exams, and you may even have to go out into the world to research special projects. As you'll see detailed later in the book, most online programs are either part of larger degree programs, or, if they're freestanding, they are noncredit or lead to credentials other than degrees. Some courses are high-tech in that they provide laptops for interaction with a professor from the back of a large lecture hall. And in some cases, sad to say, a provider may give the "Ph.D. in your pj's" come-on only to provide the true facts after your credit card is charged. (See "What to Look For" in Chapter 8 for more ideas.)

(b) *Can save a lot of education time and money.* Online education is *not* quicker, cheaper, or even easier than the traditional variety. (The firsthand experiences in Part 5 and throughout the book can show you what the actual advantages are.)

It's not quicker, because the *high-tech* in high-tech learning does not lead to some kind of time warp where an hour elapses in a few minutes. You may be able to "go to class" from your bedroom in the wee hours—but a three-hour class will still take three hours.

It's not cheaper: you can expect tuition to at least equal what you would pay on campus—and in some cases to be higher, as special fees raise the cost. (Once online courses or training programs are up and running, they *should* cost the providers less. But start-up costs are high, so these programs are even more costly to produce than bricks-and-mortar, paper-and-pencil offerings—so don't count on any cut-rate classes.)

Nor is online learning any easier than the in-person version. In fact, as you'll see from the firsthand accounts here of experienced online students, it can be more demanding. There's no snoozing in the back of the class, no dog to eat your homework, no professors who forget to show up. Those who really get into the online groove, as you can learn to do in this book, find the process a lot more stimulating than traditional modes. It even requires learning some new techniques for working with other people in your "classroom." . . . which leads to the next answer.

(c) *Will have no interaction with actual classmates or professors.* Many online students are surprised to discover that they actually have *more* contact with others than they do in flesh-and-blood classes. "For one thing, when someone asks me a question, I can't *not* answer," says a frequent training program participant. As those familiar with e-mail and chat rooms know, you can actually be more honest and intimate at a distance than face to face. And good online programs are designed to promote interaction and cooperative work. Part 6 provides inside looks at what really goes on in the virtual classroom.

Voice of Experience

"Sure I could log on anytime," says a working mom in a career course, "but when I did I had to pay *more* attention than in regular classes."

As for the teachers of online courses? Almost without exception, they report that online teaching takes more effort than standing in front of a class. One reason is that whether it's a full degree or credential program, or just a single course that instructors have chosen to put on a campus net, they need to be on call nearly 24/7 for all those highly stimulated students.

(d) *Has to be really computer-smart.* Online students do not have to be computer-smart. For one thing, there are plenty of distance programs that don't even involve computers. For another, online courses and programs that are worth taking come with high-tech how-to instructions. At a minimum, those student-friendly sites take you step by step through the hook-up process and provide software; the better ones offer special sections to evaluate your computer skills and help you to improve. (See Part 3 for ideas about that—and check out Part 7 for a speaking knowledge of this tech stuff.) Plus, you'd be surprised at how "un-sci-fi" most courses are. Once the tech tools are understood, it's a really down-to-earth (as well as close-to-home) kind of experience.

See? You've hardly even started your online education adventure, and already you're mentally putting together a list of questions to ask the provider of that course you're getting ready to take—true?

Now, for the true/false questions: all are *false.*

1. *Anyone can succeed as an online student.* Online study is *not* for everyone, and some people are unsuited for any kind of distance learning. The best online programs will give you a chance to screen yourself out. (This is discussed in Part 4.)

2. *All distance education requires a computer.* Even on-campus courses now require computers, but old-style correspondence courses are still available. You'll find details on all the types here, starting in Part 2.

3. *The best online programs are from the best-rated colleges.* The best online programs are *not* from the best or best-known colleges. Data show that public universities are more likely to offer online programs. It's also true that the traditional "Ivies" took longer to get

into the online field than less well-known schools, and unfortunately their offerings indicate that they may be relying more on their bricks-and-mortar reputations than on real value. Even the highly self-touting cyber-colleges can be more puff than program. That's why checklists like those you'll find in Part 3 and throughout the book will be important as you make your own choices for success.

4. *All distance programs give the same credentials as on-campus classes.* Distance programs may lead to the same credentials as on-campus courses, but not necessarily. Also, what counts as a credential in the state in which it's offered may not count in the state where you're studying. On the other hand, a degree achieved at a distance is not worth less than a traditionally earned degree. The work is as challenging, the faculty as demanding, and, if anything, distance learning puts more demands on the student. Many academic insiders know this, but important outsiders like employers may not accept it yet. Plus, the quality is often unequal: educational accreditation systems in many cases have not kept pace with the learning systems themselves. So it's all the more important to ask your own questions—like the ones you'll find in Chapter 8.

5. *People who have finished school won't ever need online learning.* This is something of a trick question. These days, and for the foreseeable future, there really are no people who have finished school—no halfway successful people, anyway. Twenty-first-century careers—twenty-first century lives—require constant learning, new education, and retraining.

Fast Facts

At least 75 percent of the nation's workforce will need retraining by 2010—and much of that training is ongoing: training programs are one of the fastest-growing areas of education, and soon virtually all will be delivered via high-tech media.

Demands like these have made online learning necessary, and, in turn, online educational capabilities have made lifelong learning and continual training possible. We are all perpetual students, as the discussions in Part 2 indicate. Even those who just stay at home and putter around the house need to learn new techniques. Or, they have kids who have to choose a college and may have to pick, with mom's or dad's help, which schools offer the best online opportunities.

In sum: more and more people will be studying at a distance—using some high-tech components—because:

- *This method of learning allows more students to participate, despite work and family responsibilities (well over half of the nation's college students, for example, are adults).*

- *More people must continue learning, but have schedules that prevent them from attending class.*

- *The technology for distance education continues to become simpler and more accessible.*

- *The number of students—the education market—thus grows larger and larger each semester, with the result that education is now a buyer's market: that is, students have much greater power to choose their programs than ever before. (Thus more information is needed to make an educated choice about education.)*

Voice of Experience "I'd always hoped to finish my degree," says a retired executive in Georgia. "but there was no way that, at 56, I was going to sit in a classroom with kids! Now I'm near graduating into a new career to give something back to my community."

Review your notes

To review: you need the answers you'll find in this book if you are considering study online as an undergrad; a graduate student; a returning student for credit or noncredit; a participant in a training or career certificate program, whether required by your job or chosen to get ahead on your own; a teenage college shopper; a CEO in need of high-powered training; a high school student; or the parent of a teen seeking college-level courses for advanced placement classes. If you are the parent of a student beginning the college-shopping process, you already know that your kids know more about computers than you do—but as the potential bill-payer, you need to be able to see behind the hype that even some of the most straitlaced institutions are putting forth now and ask intelligent questions about the online components of your child's high-priced education.

Or—if you're someone just itching to enter your credit card number to pay for a course that you "know" you'll love—you may really need this book.

So, whatever your interest in online learning—as a potential student by choice or necessity, as a parent of a potential student, or as someone just curious about whether online study might be for you—put your #2 pencil down for a moment and glance through this book for a preview of what you'll learn. (Previewing is a valuable study skill in any setting.) Consider this book as a critical homework tool. It provides you with the nuts and bolts of how online learning really works—and how online learners can make the most of distance education.

This book should be of greater value and interest to you and the millions of other potential online students than most books on distance learning, which are directories that list accredited colleges and universities offering distance learning—especially since that information is so readily available online. The only lists needed, participants and providers agree, are lists of Web sites that describe the providers, updated and for free, online! So this book includes those references, but goes way beyond them by actually helping everyday consumers—potential undergrads as well as graduate students and adult learners—understand how to participate in distance learning intelligently. Directories are designed to present the institutions, and an even larger number of online guides offer advice to instructors of those courses. This book, by contrast, is student focused. And we're not just talking technicalities. Yes, there are technical challenges involved with most online learning—but those challenges are no greater than trying to figure out how to find the time for school or how to find your way through registration lines and long corridors to actually get to a classroom. In any case, most providers of distance education walk you through the technical requirements of their programs (and if they don't, sign on with someone else—more on that in Chapter 8). But what even sophisticated students may not know is how, quite literally, to get along.

For instance: from childhood we're all trained in techniques designed to help us get ahead and get along in school and on the playground. Some of these techniques for success will work in this new kind of learning, but some won't. And some new techniques are needed. It's these kinds of tips that you'll find of special value as you consider working toward success in the distance education arena.

FAQs

Based on information provided by designers, teachers, and students of online or distance education programs of every type, this book should answer most of your questions about online and other types of distance learning. For those answers that you don't find here, you'll find resources for further information.

You can become an online A student by learning how to manage each type of online education—from application and registration through class participation to exams and grades. You'll find out how to manage your time and organize your study skills in this new educational venture, and you'll learn firsthand from those who know best—experienced students and actual instructors offering inside insights and success tips. You'll find profiles and anecdotes to illustrate what the distance learning experience is really like, whether delivered by computer, audio, or video, from traditional campuses, specialized training centers, or the new academic corporations.

Academic advisement professionals report that the incoming questions on online programs most frequently cover the following areas:

- Can I get a degree?
- What technology do I need?
- Does it cost less?
- Can I register online?

You'll find this to be a practical handbook for most kinds of twenty-first-century learning. Some studies still must stay in the four-walled box; most others consist of a combination of formats. But, in one form or another, distance learning, as a separate entity or as a component of other teaching techniques, is such an increasingly important element of higher education that virtually every student (pun intended) needs to develop some new school skills. This book shows how to optimize the choices—and then gain the skills that result in grade A success.

You will find the format easy to use, with checklists, questions and answers, self-tests, information bites, and fact boxes, as well as boxes highlighting the here's-how expertise of voice of experience. The book is thorough, too, with student and faculty commentary and full references to resources (including those directories and Web sites) for data on distance learning providers.

In the sections and chapters to follow, you'll find answers to these FAQs (that's *frequently asked questions*—check the glossary beginning on page 231 for these and tougher terms).

- *What is online learning?*
- *What's it like?*
- *Where can I find it?*
- *Is it for me?*
- *What works online?*
- *What makes a good candidate for online learning?*
- *What are the advantages or disadvantages for me?*
- *How do I choose an online learning provider?*
- *How do I pick a curriculum?*
- *How can I get information about sources?*
- *What makes for a good distance program?*
- *Where do I start?*
- *What do I look for?*

- *How can I succeed at a distance?*

- *How do I manage the tools and equipment?*

- *How can I best organize and manage my time?*

- *How can I develop good online study habits and work independently?*

- *How can I relate to classmates and teachers I can't see?*

- *How do I combine online learning with residential classes?*

- *How does the technology work?*

- *Where can I find the updated data I need?*

You'll not only find answers to questions like these from experts and from other distance learners surveyed for this book, but you'll have the opportunity to complete checklists that summarize the best answers for you personally.

As the book proceeds, it describes in detail what it's like to study in all of these situations, so that by the time you've gone through each step, you'll be better able to decide what type of online learning you'll be most comfortable applying for and most likely to succeed at. The following chapters are also full of specific tips on developing and applying the skills that are necessary for success in any kind of distance learning experience. So, once you've decided on a program and have been accepted into it, keep this handbook close by as a guide to your at-a-distance academic success.

Overview

Even in cyberspace, success in distance learning comes one step at a time. The next chapters cover the basics: what is distance learning? How does it work? This lays the foundation for the step-by-step process covered in subsequent chapters, including deciding whether distance learning is for you and planning how to succeed at it.

Part 2

What Is Online Study?

To earn an A from a distance, whether in college, a noncredit program, or a training course, you'll need to make some educated choices. That means having the best possible understanding of the wide variety of options available. The chapters in this part of the book provide the facts and background you need for smart decisions—describing, first, what the types of distance learning are, and then how they work. Finally, you'll have the chance to get some new ideas about where to find directions to the optimum course for you. You may be surprised by the variety of providers—and by the ease of finding them for yourself.

Chapter 2
The Types of Distance Learning

Just as the list of providers grows longer almost every minute, so the types of distance learning (DL) increase almost as quickly. There was a time (and not so long ago) when *distance learning* meant *correspondence school*. In a sense, it still does—it's just that now the correspondence is via keyboard, screen, and cyberspace, and in most cases the response is immediate.

In Other Words

Distance learning is the acquisition of knowledge and skills through mediated information and instruction. Distance learning encompasses all technologies and supports the pursuit of life long learning for all. Distance learning is used in all areas of education including Pre-K through grade 12, higher education, home school education, continuing education, corporate training, military and government training, and telemedicine.

The U.S. Department of Education

While *online learning* or *e-learning* is rapidly becoming a catch-all phrase for this kind of education, it's important to remember that there are many kinds of distance learning—it's simply any kind of learning that takes place when the instructor and student are not physically in the same space. Not everyone is suited to the high-tech variety, as you can find out for yourself, but even if you're one of those who aren't, you needn't be stuck in a four-walled classroom. As you'll learn in this chapter, there are options: learning can take place through manual, snail-mail correspondence and audio, video, or computer technologies, as well as by teleconferencing and, increasingly, via the World Wide Web (WWW), either for independent students or as part of an organized course. Usually, a mixture of techniques is used. Instruction may be synchronous (in a group, though at a distance) or asynchronous (anytime, anywhere) via the

Web or through electronic classrooms linked by telephone lines. Here, you'll find out what the different types of distance education are and what you need to receive an education at a distance. That way the high-tech buzzing won't intimidate you.

The beginnings

It may also be reassuring to remember that despite the big numbers of virtual students, distance learning is hardly a new invention. The first distance education in the United States was offered in 1728 when an ad in a Boston paper offered learning by mail. Since then, correspondence courses of all kinds have flourished. In the early twentieth century, radio was used to deliver instruction; in the 1950s, local and later national educational television became a teaching medium. Starting a few decades ago, audio- and videotapes were used to implement learning at a distance. All of those devices are still employed, of course, even while telecommunications media have taken over the distance classroom.

Where distances are greater, interest in distance learning has been historically greater. The early Americans who used those original distance instruction methods were, of course, scattered over a wider distance than their classmates in the old country. So it should come as no surprise that in the United States the higher-tech versions of distance education were established in the West and far Midwest by a consortium of universities that electronically served students scattered around the wide-open spaces.

Today, distance learning is usually (but not always!) implemented in situations where access is limited by distance or where few instructors are available to teach a widely scattered group of students. Now, though, the term *distance* doesn't necessarily mean a *far* distance. A distance learner may be located across campus from the instructor or many miles away, in another country or even on another continent—or just at the back of a classroom, using whiteboarding techniques to follow a lecture. Increasingly, the laptops needed for this kind of study are distributed by colleges to their students.

Some experts predict that distance learning tolls the end of ivied walls, expecting the bricks-and-mortar classroom to crumble under the force of cyberstudy. But it's more likely that e-learning will simply add to the choices that we have—and that we need to maintain our educational activities. We may want to go to class—but, under the new system, we will have the opportunity to also "go to class" for a course that's only offered across the continent. Likewise, the style itself offers choices: just as in a traditional setting, we can choose from among tutorials, seminars, and lecture classes. It can be a highly personalized sort of education, as providers and students are able to interact on a one-to-one basis. Or it can serve as a giant lecture hall, where 1000 or more students can receive a presentation by a leader in any given field. But today it's not just happening in universities; it's everywhere.

Learning distribution

The U.S. Department of Education defines it concisely: distance education is instructional delivery that does not constrain the student to be physically present in the same location as the instructor. Historically, distance education meant learning distributed by mail. Today, audio, video, and computer technologies are more common delivery modes. Distance learning still includes correspondence courses; it can also refer to extension classes, whereby a school or university has outposts away from its main campuses where it either holds classes or sends them via TV. These versions can be useful, of course—but they're often forgotten in our high-tech cyberstudy era (see Part 4.) More likely, our concept of distance learning includes the higher-tech varieties of education. And although the simpler versions are still around, the more sophisticated ones are changing at warp speed.

By the Numbers

According to the Department of Education, as of fall 1999, distance education courses were offered at 90 percent of colleges and universities that had enrollments of more than 10,000 students, and at 85 percent of institutions with enrollments of 3,000 to 10,000.

The definition of distance learning has changed, in part because the distance involved needn't be great: on a campus or in the cubicles of a corporation, a closed-circuit intranet may convey course content or training programs via computer messages to laptops without interrupting student schedules or employee routines. Thus, today a more useful phrase increasingly used to describe this process is *distributed learning*.

Fast Facts

Traditional universities must develop new ways to distribute their basic product—education—to nontraditional learner populations. These new learners will speak multiple languages, will live all over the world, and will be reached on remote campuses, in government and business workplaces, and directly in their own homes.

Lucent Technologies

Educators point out that there's a difference between distance learning and distance education, saying education is the job of the teacher, while learning is the responsibility of the student. Since this book focuses on the student, we'll use the term *distributed learning*. Whatever the label, DL covers all kinds of learning that are distributed by some system or technique broader perhaps than that of the words of a single teacher to the ears of an individual student. And no stereotypes actually apply. For many professional trainers, a class size of 500 is not unusual, though only one-tenth of the students may be active participants. The Learning Resource Network expects that classes of several thousand may soon be the norm; the mostly online University of Phoenix, which originally set class size at 15, found that "instructors simply could not deal with that many students," and so lowered class size to 9 students, while the all-distance Union Institute is proud of its one-on-one tutorials.

Voice of Experience

Judy Smith, an experienced online teacher and course designer, explains: "In online learning (this is different from training), the goal is to deepen the understanding. In online training, the goal is to obtain the skills via education and hopefully apply them via action learning."

Whatever your goals, the range is almost infinite, leaving you as the student the privilege of choosing what best suits you.

The human element

Just as the distribution of learning takes different forms today, so do the students who receive it. DL is, of course, used in elementary and secondary schools—but those kids don't need any help understanding the technology; they are experts from toddlerhood. That's the big reason why this kind of high-tech education isn't going to be a fad: it's the way up-and-coming students will expect to receive education. For those of us coming to the virtual classroom a bit later in life, however, it may be reassuring to know that we are not alone in our need to learn. Far from it. Statistics show that most postsecondary learners are adults. Even more so, most students signing on for distance learning are not kids by any means: rather, we enroll in order to fit education and training into our busy adult lives—education and training that we need to keep ahead of our careers. So we're not alone. In fact, we're such a big market that the providers of educational products are more than happy to ensure that we have an understanding of the equipment we'll need to participate in their offerings. The technology is not foreign, either—most of us have what it takes, technically, to become distance learners. It's just a matter of becoming informed.

Voice of Experience

DL students surveyed reported a range of high-tech experience, from "I'd never even e-mailed" to "some experience with computer applications" to "heavy user, some programming skills."

What the tools are—and what you'll need

In this section you'll find summaries of the technology that you may need to be part of a distributed learning system (for more detail, see Part 7). You'll see that some of the tools aren't quite as high-tech as you might imagine—but they may be quite prevalent for the foreseeable future. As for the more sophisticated versions, while it's not necessary to fully understand what all the tech talk is about (any more than you need to know how to program a computer in order to use it), some 3,000 colleges offer some distance learning; 450,000 training courses are offered at a distance; and new providers of educational programs are popping up on the Net almost weekly. As you explore the content and settings you want in your educational program, a speaking knowledge of the technology involved will help.

Check It Out

The forms that DL takes include:	The equipment you'll need is:
Mail (still!)	A mailbox
Video	A TV and/or VCR
Television	A TV
Radio	A radio
Videotapes	A TV and VCR
Audiotapes	A tape player
CD-ROM	A computer with a CD drive
Internet access	A computer with Internet
Streaming video	A computer with enough memory
Computerized data	A computer with appropriate software and delivery systems

Ideally, the technology used to deliver the education is only a small part of the learning experience; it should disappear into the background, just as classroom walls and furniture do. Though the technology should become only a tool, like a blackboard and chalk, your familiarity with it is likely to increase your comfort and help it to disappear.

Both experts and students agree that distance learning *must* be more about learning than about technology. But a basic knowledge of the technical tools is as important to a learner as a basic knowledge of the workings of a car is to a driver.

The tools

Following are descriptions of the most common media by which your new learning may be distributed. The descriptions here should indicate the variety of resources, of course—but, more importantly, they should demonstrate that you needn't be a high-tech wizard to sign on for online learning. Here and in the next chapter, you'll get enough information to ask intelligent questions. Just as a driver wants some expertise but needn't know how to build an engine, or a personal computer (PC) user doesn't have to know how to program a computer, a distance student needs some knowledge of the technology—if only to know what questions to ask.

To start, distance learning may be (1) asynchronous or (2) synchronous. Those ten-dollar words, which are derived from ancient Greek roots, simply mean (1) not (*a*) at the same (*syn*) time (*chron*) and (2) at the same (*syn*) time (*chron*).

Asynchronous instruction does not require the simultaneous participation of all students and instructors. Students do not need to be gathered together in the same location at the same time. Forms of asynchronous delivery include e-mail, listservs, audiocassette courses, videotaped courses, correspondence courses, and WWW-based courses.

Synchronous instruction requires the simultaneous participation of all students and instructors, with interaction taking place in real time. Forms of synchronous delivery include interactive TV, audiographics, computer conferencing, IRC, MOOs, MUDs, and, more recently, some Web courses.

MOOs, MUDs, IRC, es, and servs—YIKES! Translation, please!

Tech talk

Actually, it's pretty simple. In addition to the printed word (which, of course, can arrive by fax as well as by human delivery), there are just a few electrical and electronic media through which learning takes place over distance: audio, video, and computer. You'll note that not all of these are online: that's just one subcategory of computer-based learning, and one that has a variety of aspects, as you'll learn.

Here are the basics. Distance learning can be distributed via:

Voice. This includes such interactive media as telephone, audioconferencing, and shortwave radio, and passive (one-way) tools like tapes and radio.

Video. These tools range from still images, like slides, through film or videotape to real-time (live), moving images. It may include audioconferencing, which is a two-way or interactive technology that uses, for example, one-way or two-way video with two-way audio.

Data. Computers send and receive information electronically, and the data can be communicated via various computer applications, including:

★ *Computer-assisted instruction (CAI), where the computer is a self-contained teaching machine to present individual lessons. [CAI is also known as computer-based training (CBT).]*

★ *Computer-managed instruction (CMI), where the computer organizes instruction and student records and progress whether or not the instruction itself is delivered via computer.*

★ *Computer-mediated education (CME), in which computer applications facilitate instruction using electronic mail, fax, real-time computer conferencing, and World Wide Web applications.*

And then of course, there's print. Print?! Yes . . . printed materials are at least as important in even high-tech distance learning as they are in the traditional varieties. In addition to the fact that curricula begin with written words, students working at a distance from each other and the teacher have a great need for in-print instructions, texts, and workbooks.

Most courses combine techniques and become *hybrids,* making them a bit more complicated to understand. How much technological detail you'd like to grasp is up to you. Some drivers of cars, after all, want to know only how to turn the key; others need to be able to take a car apart. Some computer users need to know only where the start button is and the number of their tech support line—others need to program and reprogram their devices. Here are some basics. What counts, of course—and what your course provider should explain (see Chapter 8)—is what you'll need to make it work.

In Other Words

High-tech words may be impressive—but this is how to break them down, just as you used to in vocabulary studies for those standardized tests: the parts come from ancient (and not-so-ancient) languages.

video. ("I see") Delivered by eye.

audio. ("I hear") Delivered by ear.

digit. ("finger") Delivered by computer.

tele-. ("far") From a distance (television—seen from a distance; teleconferencing—meeting from a distance).

e-. Shorthand for *electronic,* as in electronically transmitted mail, learning, commerce, etc.

online. Delivered directly by electronic means (as compared with prerecorded software provided on disk).

What you'll need

Following is what you'll need to participate in the different forms of telelearning. To receive audio- or video-based programs, you'll need, of course, a TV, VCR, or tape deck—but you'll want to be sure in advance that when course providers say *audio,* they really mean tape. Most of us have these devices in our homes—but it's also possible to go to a library and make use of equipment there. While it is of course convenient to have it all at home, it's worth noting that by visiting libraries on campus or off-campus centers, you can take advantage of asynchronous learning without laying out big bucks.

Video-provided courses may require only a TV and VCR, or they may require special lines to connect you. They may be as simple as a videotape, or as complex as uniquely designed programs transmitted by satellite to one site or many. Video learning includes:

Telecourses. These are a series of video tapes accompanied by textbooks and study guides focusing on a given subject.

One-way video. This is traditional educational TV. It is often combined with audio return, enabling students to interact with the teacher and students at other sites by telephone (audioconferencing) or fax.

Two-way video. This system uses digital transmission systems, such as digital telephone lines, to bring teacher and remote student into, if not the same classroom, then a real-time multimedia experience—interactive video conferencing (IVC) via a two-way auditory and visual communication.

Video teleconference: In this distance learning medium, students and faculty meet at the same time and can see and talk to each other using video cameras, microphones, and the Internet or telephone lines to connect the sites.

Computer-provided programs require a computer, of course—one with enough memory to handle the operations required—and that may be all. Or, special lines and special features such as CD-ROM drives might be needed to handle the special disks that may contain programs and course materials.

The first step in preparing for an online education is thus to be sure you have the right equipment. The provider should explain all that to you in advance and at least help you to find what you need. The electronic connection as well will need to meet the requirements of the course delivery system. (For instance, in some areas, even telephone communication is rare, so electronic distance learning may be impossible!)

The data—or electronically coded information bits that make up high-tech courses—has to get to you. Data moves by telephone lines to modems (remember to see the glossary to define unfamiliar terms). But that method can be slow, so new connections have been developed. For instance, Integrated Services Digital Network (ISDN) lines are phone lines that move data digitally—a much faster way of transmitting than traditional phone lines and modems—to reduce access and download times for WWW pages and File Transfer Protocol (FTP) files. Digital Subscriber Line (DSL) and Asymmetric Digital Subscriber Line (ASDL) are new types of data communication lines that deliver and receive information on the current telephone lines at a much greater speed. These also require special installation by the phone company. All of these special connections may not be necessary—but it's important to find that out ahead of time.

You will need a modem that allows you to connect and "converse" electronically via e-mails or listservs. (Listservs are electronic mailing lists that allow you to send the same information to many people by addressing a message to a single computer. The computer forwards the message to everyone on the list—a few others or thousands of individuals. For distance learning, the entire class might be on a listserv for a discussion.)

Teleconferencing

Teleconferencing is the use of electronic channels to facilitate communication among groups of people at two or more locations via audio, video, or computer. *Teleconferencing* is the generic term that refers to a variety of technologies and applications, including audioconferencing, videoconferencing, and computer conferencing. *Audioconferencing* and *videoconferencing* refer to two-way voice or visual communication between two or more groups or three or more individuals in separate locations. *Computer conferencing* is the use of electronic channels to facilitate communication among groups of people at two or more locations via computer. Computer conferencing includes Internet Relay Chat (IRC), Multi-user Object-Oriented environments (MOOs), and Multi-User Domains (MUDs) as tools to share information and images.

IRC is Internet software that allows real-time electronic conversations between hundreds of users. IRC has different channels, each of which contains a separate conversation. You can move between channels and send messages from channel to channel. A MOO is an environment that allows real-time (that is, instantaneous—not a message posted and responded to) communication over the Internet. With a MOO, you connect to a host via Telnet and land in a virtual room, and you can converse with anyone else who has connected to the same host and who shares that room with you. You can also move from room to room, and you can page people who are in other rooms. A MUD is a version of a MOO that uses only text, while a MOO incorporates pictures.

Internet-based programs are found on the Web and contain detailed information about and content for a course. They are self-contained in that the student does not meet in person with other learners or the instructor. Communication occurs through e-mail, listservs, MOOs, threaded discussions, and chat rooms. Most assignments and tests are completed and submitted online.

Hybrids

These days, this kind of communication has become too sophisticated for one technology alone, so most systems are *hybrids,* or mixtures. For these, you will need a wider variety of equipment. For example, *audiographics* is the combined use of voice transmission, computer networking, and graphics transmission through narrowband telecommunications channels. Connections can be made using standard telephone lines or digital communication lines. Graphics can be transmitted by facsimile (fax) machine, still video systems, computers (text or graphic display), or electronic drawing systems (such as electronic blackboards), which allow you to draw or write on an electronic screen that is transmitted to a remote site where other participants may see it.

In other hybrid environments, a video course may also have a course Web site, a Web-based course may use video and audio clips to enhance delivery, and both interactive video and Web-based courses may incorporate streaming video or real-time video and audioconferencing via the Internet or via speakerphone into the course design.

For added depth of definition, check the resources at the back of the book.

Which delivery system fits best with technology you already have and/or are familiar and comfortable with? Use this guide.

	TV	VCR	AUDIOTAPES	COMPUTER	MODEM	SPECIAL LINES
Checklist						
Equipment I have						
Budget I have to add						
What I'm comfortable with						

As you can see, while you may have TV and/or VCR and/or computer and/or telephone lines, you'll need them in the right combination to fit the program offered.

Which technology is best?

Should you judge a program by its technology? Probably not (though there's more discussion of this in Chapter 8). It's just that it's important to be clear about the equipment you'll need to receive the course material. Is one technology better than another? Not necessarily, according to those who are experts in the theory and application of distance learning delivery. Rather, technologies are tools that enable the instructor and the learner to interact—and the more you can interact with the instructor and your classmates, studies show, the more satisfying and successful will be your online educational experience.

The best technology may be, in fact, a combination of several technologies for different purposes. Which is best for you? It really depends on which is best for your comfort level and for the coursework you're seeking. In the next chapter you will find some descriptions of how the technologies work, and the different experiences real-life students have with each type. Technology is just the tool that distributes the learning. Putting it to use brings this kind of learning to life.

Chapter 3

How the Types of Distance Learning Work

Terms like *virtual classroom, e-learning,* and MOO *environments* call to mind a sci-fi scene of goggled space explorers and eerie blue light. Actually, the reality of distance and even online learning is a lot more down to earth. That is, the TVs, VCRs, computers, and fax machines that are a part of your daily life are now the tools of your learning experience.

The better the tools, the smoother the learning. Just as learning in the classroom is more effective if the student is more than a passive listener at a lecture, so the best tools are those that allow for interaction, even at a distance. In fact, there are those who say that learning via computer is more effective than the face-to-face variety.

Fast Facts

Dozens of studies conducted over the last half-century have shown no significant difference between the results of distance and of in-class education. In fact, more recent studies show that online classes can be more successful than traditional courses when they allow for active engagement and interaction. In fact, since any kind of distance education requires special student initiative, it's automatically more engaging.

Into action

It may well be true that "a top misconception about distance education is that it's the use of a particular kind of technology," as Daniel Granger, director of distance learning at the University of Minnesota's Virtual University College, notes, and that the focus should be on the education rather than modems, computers, video, satellites, or interactive TV.

Still, going to class for the first time, ever since that first day of kindergarten, can bring butterflies to the stomach—and even virtual butterflies can be uncomfortable. So, when you go to the virtual classroom, having some knowledge of what the technological aspects are will make it more comfortable.

In Other Words

As the U.S. Department of Education puts it, "Programming for distance learning provides the receiver many options both in technical configurations and content design. Educational materials are delivered primarily through live and interactive classes. The intent of these programs is not necessarily to replicate face-to-face instruction. Interactivity is accomplished via telephone (one-way video and two-way audio), two-way video or graphics interactivity, two-way computer hookups, or response terminals."

Here's what it's really like. Check out some examples of what the educational technology is like in action. Visualize this: you're home—after (or before) a day's work. Or you're *at* work. Or it's the middle of the night. Or it's a sunny Sunday afternoon. You're in your . . . pajamas/business suit/bikini. You turn on your TV (or VCR, or fax machine, or computer) and enter your password (the one you got after you paid for the program!), and learning begins.

What learning is like by TV

You may turn on the set at a prearranged time or put a videotape into the VCR to view preproduced programs. Or, a TV can become interactive: two-way television with two-way audio allows students to view and interact with the teacher. At the same time, cameras at remote sites allow the teacher to view all participating students. It is also possible to configure the system so that all student sites may view one another. In the interactive visual communications (IVC) classroom, you're in a remote classroom with other students, viewing an instructor whose image is sent by a TV camera from a delivery site and who demonstrates points via a digital camera.

Picture This

In a one-way TV classroom, you and fellow students at remote sites can see the teacher on a television monitor, but the teacher cannot see you. You ask questions by phone, fax, or FM radio during class, and sometimes by e-mail—but a teaching assistant on-site is also available. The classroom can be interactive via fax and computer.

TV, whether at home or in the classroom, has advantages because it is such a familiar medium. Also, it can (when well done) convey messages, concepts, and information more effectively than in-person or digital lectures.

Picture This

You're in a chat room talking to other students by typing in messages on your computer. The writing appears immediately on each participant's screen, so you can use these rooms [via Internet Relay Chat (IRC) or Web software] for discussions and team or group work. You might also be in contact by a computer conference—a discussion group for students that is organized to follow a topic from start to finish, but that doesn't happen in real time: rather, you read and make comments over a period of time.

Then there's streaming video (or audio). Via a video stream, your computer turns multimedia: you view—and participate in—images that move through your computer as though you are watching a movie.

What learning is like by VCR

You've put your packaged supper in the microwave; now you turn on the TV and VCR, insert a tape, and pull out your telecourse workbook. At your own pace, you can view a series of videotapes and get your lessons on a given topic with the help of a textbook and study guide.

What learning is like by audio tape, radio, or interactive media

Pick up your phone and go to class in interactive audio- or videoconferencing modes that can provide real-time face-to-face (or voice-to-voice) interaction. Audio-only conferencing typically uses the public telephone system to link together people at two or more locations. (For larger groups, additional equipment can be used to reduce noise and interference.) Technical components of an audio-only conference might include telephone handsets, speakerphones, or microphones; an audio bridge that interconnects multiple phone lines and controls noise; and a speaker device to facilitate multiple interactions. While your phone can be an e-teaching tool, these days it's usually part of a bigger system combining voice communications, computer networking, and graphics transmission. Interactive video conferencing, a two-way auditory and visual communication system that allows users to see the sites and people to which they are connected, offers an added advantage over standard one-way video communication mechanisms such as satellite transmission.

Picture This

In an audio- or videographic classroom, your computer becomes a blackboard. Though you can't see the instructor or your classmates, the teacher uses a digital drawing pad and keyboard to produce graphics that immediately appear on your screen. You and other students can respond via your own drawing pads or by speakerphone. Fax machines are also used to transmit tests and other hard copy.

What learning is like by computer

You can use these (for most) familiar tools—like e-mail—to send to and receive from one or more class members messages, assignment feedback, and other targeted communications. Some distance education courses are offered entirely via e-mail, while others combine several delivery modes, using e-mail for increased interactivity among individuals or listservs for large numbers of users.

Visualize this: you power up your computer (and these days, you can be on a train or plane as well as in the office as you plug into class using your laptop or an even smaller unit). Wherever you are, and whatever your computer looks like, it's become a powerful tool in all varieties of distributed learning. Asynchronous learning networks (ALNs) combine self-study with rapid, real, anytime/anywhere interactivity with others. In ALNs, learners use computer and communications technologies to work according to their own schedules. While some distance learning courses have many synchronous features—scheduled online meetings, or satellite broadcasts that are only shown once—most schools are including asynchronous elements in their distance learning courses. Lectures and assignments are posted to a class Web site, and students come to them when it's most convenient—from chat room discussions to e-mail and even online audio and video. When you are in an asynchronous virtual classroom, software on a Web server creates a virtual place and shows a professor presenting the course content and facilitating discussion. It's usually possible not only to get your course online, but to register, order books, send papers, and even take tests at a distance.

Which computer-based distance education system appeals most to you?

- **Computer-assisted instruction (CAI).** In this system, the computer is a self-contained teaching machine that presents lessons for specific but limited educational objectives, such as drill and practice, tutorials, simulations and games, and problem solving.

- **Computer-managed instruction (CMI).** Here the computer's connection, storage, and retrieval capabilities organize instruction and track student records and progress. This system is often, but not always, combined with CAI.

- **Computer-mediated communication (CMC).** Here the computer facilitates communication, as in electronic mail, computer conferencing, and electronic bulletin boards.

- **Computer-based multimedia.** This system uses HyperCard, hypermedia, and rapidly developing categories of tools to integrate voice, video, and computer technologies into a single, easily accessible delivery system for individual or group use. When combined with TV or radio, it facilitates *streaming* or real-time video or audio, allowing for the direct connection of a source to a recipient via computer.

Professor Daniel Price of the Union Institute describes a real student's life thanks to a virtual environment:

> . . . the experience of Jessica R. who lives and works in Juneau, AK. She works full-time as a counselor in an alcohol clinic, and she uses a wheel-chair which makes regular attendance all the more difficult, so she has chosen to complete her degree through a distant learning program, using the Internet as well as CD-ROMs and various software packages.
>
> Jessica does her schoolwork according to her personal schedule, day or night, seven days a week. She logs onto the computer and receives assignments, uploads files, conducts research, enters chat rooms—all at her own timetable and convenience. She has the option of location, again depending on schedule and convenience—home, office, or a hotel room while at workshops, or the guest bedroom when visiting parents at Seattle. From any of these locations she can more than simply do "homework" assignments as she would if attending a traditional program. She actually "goes to school" since she pulls down the latest class discussion, receives and posts assignments, and interacts with her professors, her classmates, her advisor. She even registers and pays her bills from any of these locations.
>
> In choosing her courses, Jessica has the option of utilizing the world library that lists hundreds of courses from dozens of institutions around the world. Although she could plan all of her degree program with multiple offerings from multiple schools, she has chosen to concentrate on only two accredited colleges. Also, since Jessica is not limited to one time slot or to one campus she has more options regarding the instructors for the courses she is selecting. Currently Jessica is working with an instructor in San Diego, another in Boston, a third in Houston while her classmates from across the country are working with faculty likewise in several locations.

What learning is like by the internet

As more and more colleges, universities, schools, companies, and private citizens connect to the Internet—which is simply a massive computer network—more and more opportunities open for distance learning. With access to the Internet, you and your teachers can communicate by electronic mail (e-mail) to exchange messages or other information with people via software through a computer network to a computer address, or via bulletin boards—like Usenet and listservs—topically organized discussion forums on a variety of subjects.

Voice of Experience

This is my second semester online. I used to live nearby, where I began attending the community college; I then moved back to my hometown, so it is hard for me to get to campus more than once a week. I now enjoy online courses, especially since I am a new father of a son who is now a year and a half old. I enjoy spending time with my family and reading. I do not have a concrete major yet, but I am leaning toward psychology. I originally signed up for the course because it was open, but after I went online and read what the course was about in detail, I think I will learn a lot.

A distance education student in New York

The World Wide Web (WWW) provides Internet users with a uniform and convenient means of accessing a wide variety of media (pictures, text, data, sound, video). Software interfaces, such as Mosaic and Netscape, are used to facilitate navigation and use of the WWW. Distance learning based on the Web is self-contained in that the student does not meet in person with other learners or the instructor. Communication occurs through e-mail, listservs, multi-user object-oriented environments (MOOs), threaded discussions, and chat rooms. Through MOOs, students with modems can connect to campus computers, Telnet to the MOO site, and join their classmates in synchronous discussions, viewing slides, and accessing other virtual objects to incorporate into their learning.

Synchronous conferencing enables students at different sites to interact and collaborate. Every student in the class can connect at the same time to the same virtual room, or students in smaller groups can meet in separate rooms. An instructor/moderator can be online to guide the process. This makes distance learning comfortable for people who learn better in groups.

Picture This

You might find yourself juggling hybrid courses. Combining various technologies for course delivery, an IVC course may also have a course Web site. A Web based course may use video and audio clips to enhance delivery. In addition, both IVC and Web based courses may incorporate streaming video and audio technologies and/or audio conferencing, via the Internet or speakerphone, into the course design.

Here's how the University of Maryland University College (UMUC), a leading distance learning institution for many years, summarizes how different types of distance classrooms work.

In what they label a distributed classroom . . .

. . . Interactive telecommunications technologies extend a classroom-based course from one location to a group of students at one or more other locations; the typical result is an extended "section" that mixes on-site and distant students. The faculty and institution control the pace and place of instruction.

Class sessions involve synchronous communication; students and faculty are required to be in a particular place at a particular time (once a week at a minimum). Number of sites varies from two (point-to-point) to five or more (point-to-multipoint); the greater the number of sites, the greater the complexity—technically, logistically, and perceptually.

Students may enroll at sites more convenient to their homes or work locations than the campus. Institutions are able to serve small numbers of students in each location.

The nature of the experience mimics that of the classroom for both the instructor and the student. The technology it employs includes: two-way interactive video, one-way video with two-way audio, audioconferencing, and audiographic conferencing. External communication is by telephone, mail, fax, and computer.

There is another system that they term "Independent Learning" . . .

. . . This model frees students from having to be in a particular place at a particular time. Students are provided a variety of materials, including a course guide and detailed syllabus, and access to a faculty member who provides guidance, answers questions, and evaluates their work. Contact between the individual student and the instructor is achieved by one or a combination of the following technologies: telephone, voice-mail, computer conferencing, electronic mail, and regular mail. There are no class sessions; students study independently, following the detailed guidelines in the syllabus. Presentation of course content is through print, computer disk, or videotape, all of which students can review at a place and time of their own choosing. Course materials are used over a period of several years, and generally are the result of a structured development process that involves instructional designers, content experts, and media specialists not specific to a particular instructor. Students and instructors may communicate by mail, phone, voice-mail, or computer.

There's also what they call "Open Learning + Classtime" . . .

. . . This model involves the use of a printed course guide and other media (such as videotape or computer disk) to allow the individual student to study at his or her own pace, combined with occasional use of interactive telecommunications technologies for group meetings among all enrolled students.

Presentation of course content is through print, computer disk, or videotape, all of which students can review at a place and time of their own choosing, either individually or in groups.

Course materials (for content presentation) are used for more than one semester; often specific to the particular instructor (e.g., a videotape of the instructor's lectures). Students come together periodically in groups in specified locations for instructor-led class sessions through interactive technologies (following the distributed classroom model).

Class sessions are for students to discuss and clarify concepts and engage in problem-solving activities, group work, laboratory experiences, simulations, and other applied learning exercises.

Technology used includes two-way interactive video, one-way video with two-way audio, audioconferencing, or audiographic conferencing, and external communication is through phone, computer, and mail.

Voice of Experience

Here's how Karen Coffey, a professor at Monroe Community College, Rochester, New York, explains her course procedure to her class (some of whom are neighbors, some across the state, and some overseas).

I expect you to do the following:

- Log-on, replicating the databases at least three times a week. This will allow you to stay up to date on all new input to the discussions as well as any new email or bulletin board messages.

- Respond to discussion questions within the time frame indicated. I'm looking for responses that show some real thought rather than empty words.

- Turn in or complete all writing assignments and tests when they are due. I look for proper English usage, with standard formal grammar and spelling utilized. I can preview all assignments for content . . .

The point of it all

As more and more students are receiving their education via high-tech means, it's useful to remember that the method of delivery affects more than simple convenience. It's becoming clear that the medium makes a significant—and for the student, usually positive—impact on education itself. These new formats can make learning more effective.

Voice of Experience

Here's how students in various settings actually experienced distributed learning.

"There was an online chat session to allow us to better use the biweekly chat function . . ."

"I didn't expect to learn as much—but the readings and written assignments made up for loss of class time."

"The time for assignments is demanding, but probably no more so than a traditional class. Class activities consist of a biweekly chat room. . . ."

"I participate when my work schedule allows it. . . ."

"I travel with my work quite a bit and an asynchronous Internet class is the best way for me . . ."

William Draves, director of the national Learning Resource Network and writer on learning and teaching at a distance, summarizes what the new education configurations mean for students: they can "reread a unit, review a video, and retest themselves. A learner can focus on specific content areas. . . . With online learning, we as learners can focus more time, attention and energy on those units, modules or sections of the course where we need the most help and learning. A learner can test him- or herself daily. With online learning, a learner can take quizzes and tests easily, instantly receiving the results . . ."

Technology can be not just a convenience, but a plus in learning. As the Center for the Study of Distance Learning reports, studies showed positive gains in student learning when combinations of teaching media and various methods of instruction were linked to use of technology. For example, students using computer conferencing technology evaluate each other's work, or they work in teams on larger projects. The interaction of collaborative work and technology often produces positive results in student achievement.

Technology brings more than convenient research modes to a student. The kind of active learning it promotes has long been considered one of the most effective learning methods. This kind of learning, notes Daniel Price, is particularly suited to electronic means. The use of hypertext links encourages the learner to be actively involved in his or her own learning, since it requires a constant series of choices about the next step for learning. One principle of active learning is that the learner moves at his or her own pace and does not necessarily "begin at the beginning." If a learner starts at one place, it is easy enough through the use of hypertext to go backward or forward or sideways. So there can be many advantages to studying online—and, once you come to understand the use of technology, it can be a smooth experience as well.

In the glossary in Part 7 of this book, you'll find detailed descriptions of many technical terms and systems. The chapters in Part 5 will help you explore in depth how to make optimal use of these new learning systems.

But whether the focus is on content, processes, or technology, what really matters is that you are moving toward your educational goals. Most students interviewed who are succeeding with online learning are also having little if any difficulty with the technology involved. But it's important to remember that the machine you're using—whether it's a computer, VCR, or TV—is not the source of your education. Where does the education come from? We'll learn more about the providers in the next chapters.

Chapter 4
Who Provides Distance Learning?

Despite the high-tech buzz about virtual campuses, it's surely at least as important to know who is sending the edu-signals as how you're picking them up. These days, figuring it out may be more complicated than you might imagine, because long-distance learning is so "in" that almost every provider of almost any kind of instruction, education, or training hopes to hook us into some kind of independent study. Who's really on the other side of that computer screen? The variety of providers, combined with their collection of labels and aliases, can be baffling. In the following pages, you'll be able to glean an idea of the possibilities, and in the boxes and sidebars you'll find some examples of the variety that is presenting itself to a sometimes puzzled public.

Where to find distributed learning

Students can find courses to suit from some traditional providers, but even more so from newer entrants into the education field. In fact, the old-school institutions are scrambling to catch up with the upstarts.

You can find at least 100,000 courses (it's hard to keep count because the number keeps growing) at the approximately 4,000 U.S. higher education institutions:

Public colleges
　Two-year
　Four-year

Public universities
Private colleges
  Two-year
  Four-year
Private universities

Many of these are on-campus intranet offerings that are part of more traditional programs, but more and more are being offered (for credit or not) to wider student bodies. The public sector provides more than the private sector, and began sooner, though the private schools are catching up. This is an area where two-year institutions like community and junior colleges took the lead in providing innovative material.

Voice of Experience

Did you specifically seek an online course?

Yes, but I live an hour's drive from the nearest university which offers the courses I needed.

How did you decide what course or program to sign on for? What questions did you ask?

I had some specific criteria that had to be met; my goal was to be able to sit for the CPA exams in Alaska. I wanted something accredited so it would be recognized by the state. I wanted a fast program, because I've been in post-secondary education for almost seven years now. In addition, if possible, I wanted a second bachelor's degree. UMUC offered all of these.

What guidelines were offered about your suitability for program?

Little in the way of guidelines were offered on the Internet. The program looked good, and came through an established University system (U. of Maryland), which to me was very important.

What questions should you have asked?

If I could have asked about the quality of the program before signing up, I would have. However, I started with one class in the summer of 1999 and have been satisfied with the program so far, for the most part.

What kind of training did you receive before beginning to take or teach courses?

There was a guide for beginners on how to use UMUC's particular system (WebTycho), but I didn't have time to go through it. I found that UMUC's system was very easy to work with.

High schools and grade schools use e-learning within the walls of their schools and also via internet hookups to bring the universe of learning directly into their classrooms. The nation's graduate schools and professional schools are increasingly online, or offer programs with online components, although they were a little slower to come on board.

> Higher education consortiums
> Public
> Private

To date, at least a few public colleges in each region of the country have forged these higher education links, with others in the works. Public school systems are linking up as well, so that more schools can take advantage of specialized teachers and curricula in other parts of the state or country. Private institutions are also connecting to ease the transfer of credits among them.

Western Governors University (WGU), for example, calls itself "a unique institution that offers degrees and certificates that make it possible for you to accelerate your 'time to degree' by providing recognition for your expertise. It is a new kind of higher education institution that uses technology to reach students wherever they are . . ." WGU says that it is "the first virtual university to combine the distance education classes of traditional colleges and universities with the classes designed by corporations and publishers into one comprehensive catalog, drawing on a teaching faculty that is distributed at dozens of institutions." (In that description of itself, WGU also noted that, at the time, it was not accredited. That's why the list of questions to ask in Chapter 8 is so important!)

Distance learning began with correspondence courses from for-profit trade and training schools. Today, this is one of the fastest-growing areas of distributed learning. For-profit educational institutions represent a more complex mix, including

> Private trade and training schools
> "Dot-com" universities

Here, you can find programs in almost anything you might want to learn, with almost as wide a variety in quality and price.

In Other Words

Online training expert Brandon Hall explains:

Learning Portals are web sites that provide a combination of courses, collaboration and community. Initially set up with e-commerce for the individual purchaser with a credit card, most portals have plans to offer credits of some type for multiple registrations from a single organization. The most likely winning model: the aggregators who offer courses from multiple content creators. Like Amazon.com for books, they want to be the single place you go on the Internet to find the training you want.

Continuing education schools, the lifelong learning divisions of universities, are descendants of the original extension schools—the higher education arms devoted to outreach and practical education for citizens in outlying regions. They have historically provided flexible training and educational programs designed to meet the needs of working adult students—and they are catching up fast in offering the higher-tech forms of distributed learning. The University Continuing Education Association (at www.nucea.edu) lists several hundred of these higher education connected providers, and the nation's 2000 or so community colleges offer continuing education online.

You'll also find lifelong learning opportunities at a distance from:

> Libraries
> Museums
> Associations

that provide special-interest programs in their fields of expertise—mostly to their own members, but increasingly to the public at large. Most of these are noncredit, but increasingly these providers are linking with colleges and other providers to support for-credit offerings.

Likewise, many corporations, large and small, are making use of distance learning—at first only internally, to provide training for their employees scattered around the country and the world, or just in their office buildings. Increasingly they're packaging information for delivery to the public as well.

When these and all the other specific-topic training programs are added up, they total an estimated 450,000 online or otherwise high-tech courses. The American Society of Training Directors (ASTD) provides training via some form of at-a-distance delivery, designed and provided by expert trainers in thousands of specialized fields.

This review of dozens of types of providers has not yet included the multiplying-too-fast-to-count

Online courses

offered by freestanding course providers that, for a fee, offer non-credit learning on a wide range of topics at mushrooming clusters of dot-com Web sites, some of which were developed simply in order to offer easy-access learning. These courses are usually provided by anonymous trainers. But, at increasing numbers of other sites, learning is the "come-on"—the product dangled to intrigue visitors onto an otherwise for-profit e-commerce site.

Finally, that item does not include

Packaged programs

Private companies create what some call "canned education"—courses that are contracted out to existing, older-line educational institutions. ed2go.com, eCollege.com, and Blackboard are a few of these packagers. They may help an institution put up its own courses, or they may simply provide a course for the university to present. The quality and content may (or may not) be fine; the providers are usually anonymous, and may or may not be connected with the college you've enrolled in (more reasons to ask those questions in Chapter 8!). These courses can be viewed as a way to expand a college's offerings (or make its online offerings more interesting than the standard lecture)—or as just a way to allow those institutions to include an important "online" category in their catalogs.

....

In Other Words

Follow the dots

Though ID's can change at cyberspeed, here are some tips on who's providing the course you're considering. Use the section following the dot in the World Wide Web (www) or e-mail address as a clue.

name.edu indicates an educational institution or group such as a school, college, or teachers' group.

name.org represents other types of nonprofit providers such as associations or cultural institutions.

name.gov comes from a governmental body of some kind, usually a local, state, or federal information resource.

name.com indicates a commercial, for-profit venture—even if a name like *school* or *Harvard* precedes the dot-com.

....

To illustrate

Who provides distance learning? As you can see, the answer is not as obvious as it might seem. Outside packagers may supply programs to established providers; established providers might distribute "artificial" versions of their courses. The standard professor in front of the class may be jazzed up with theatrics—or may not, and may be boring.

Putting a course online involves a lot more than sitting a teacher at a computer and sending out the curriculum. On the one hand, some providers are amateurs who do not know how to package a course. On the other, some courses are provided by, frankly, packagers. Sometimes, these canned goods may be taught by respected professors from major universities; increasingly, however, colleges are taking action to limit this practice, or at least to keep their own teachers at their own sites.

Fast Facts

Some headline stories illustrate the newly emerging shape of twenty-first-century higher education, as seen by the *Chronicle of Higher Education:*

> . . . The media baron Rupert Murdoch has linked his giant News International company with the 18-member university network Universitas 21 in a move designed to capture the major share of the rapidly growing global market for online higher education . . .
>
> CLOSELY WATCHED UNEXT ROLLS OUT ITS FIRST COURSES UNext.com, the high-profile and well-financed online-learning venture announced last year, is testing its first courses . . . provided through a new subsidiary called Cardean University, an institution created by UNext to award degrees and credits . . . UNext's higher-education partners, which are supplying the course content, include Carnegie Mellon, Columbia, and Stanford Universities, the University of Chicago, and the London School of Economics and Political Science. The company—which has attracted such investors as Michael Milken, the financier, and Larry Ellison, chief executive officer of Oracle Corporation—eventually plans to sell to the public a range of courses in business, engineering, and writing, but for now is focusing on students who are employed by its business partners. *For now, UNext's 50 or so students can choose from four business courses . . . taught by adjunct professors hired directly by UNext.* [Italics added.]

In every area of education provision, issues of quality, content, branding, and marketability may influence the kinds of programs an organization or site may offer, but, in general, different providers are likely to offer their own types of programs at a distance. Here are some examples of the new kind of education offered by all those "old-fashioned" institutions:

Public colleges
> Two-year
> Four-year

Public universities

Private colleges
> Two-year
> Four-year

As well as the more recent arrivals to the educational scene:

For-profit educational institutions

Trade and training schools

Dot-com universities

The higher education hierarchy is being stood on its head—not only are students increasingly at the control panels, but the providers that were once looked down upon are now in the forefront. For example: continuing education has new status in the eyes of campus faculty. Long considered second-rate providers of "night school" courses, continuing education units are now being seen as pioneers in the delivery of education to new markets via new technologies. It's a whole new landscape. Use these examples as the landmarks on the road map to a brave new world of learning.

Private universities and graduate schools are getting into the act—for example, the Internet Master of Business Administration program at various universities, provided through eCollege.com.

Voice of Experience

In contrast with the provision of education as a multimedia experience, many leading universities still just install cameras in lecture halls to turn professors' monologues into Webcasts. Even when these, like Harvard's, are presented through such cutting-edge technologies as streaming video, this approach is less than optimum. "They take a physics class with 1000 kids falling asleep and think if it goes online it's going to be exciting," notes Roger Schank, director of Northwestern University's Institute for Learning Sciences. As high-tech start-ups rewrite the rules, can colleges move fast enough to keep up?

• •

Increasingly, you'll find collaborative ventures, like the Collaboration for Interactive Visual Distance Learning (CIVDL), a unique association of businesses and universities that have used distance learning technology to create a virtual campus. CIVDL offers high-level technical instruction and advanced degree programs directly in the workplace from such educational institutions as Boston University, Columbia University, Howard University, the Massachusetts Institute of Technology (MIT), Penn State, Rensselaer Polytechnic Institute, and Stanford University. Current industry partners in the CIVDL group include AT&T, 3M, United Technologies Corporation, and PictureTel.

Professional schools such as the National Technological University (NTU) provide lifelong learning for engineering professionals. NTU provides more than 27,000 annual programming hours of advanced engineering degree programs. NTU's courses originate from more than 40 major higher education institutions.

Even in grade schools, electronic networking is in. In one example, a group of seven school districts in northeastern Wisconsin called the Embarrass River Valley Instructional Network Group (ERVING), is using a network of fiber-optic circuits and interactive video classrooms for distance learning. This network allows the schools to pool instructional resources to offer expanded curricula for learners, staff development programs for instructors, and adult education opportunities for community members. Each classroom on the network is equipped with cameras, monitors, microphone systems, VCRs, phones, and fax machines. The fiber-optic network uses AT&T 45-Mbps technology to deliver television-quality video and CD-quality audio. All sites can originate and receive programs.

You can get plenty of education right off your television. The Public Broadcasting Service (PBS) offers nationwide educational programs such as PBS MATHLINE and the Adult Learning Satellite Service (ALSS), which provides undergraduate-level courses and resources programming to over 2000 colleges, universities, hospitals, and other organizations throughout the country that are equipped with satellite receiver capabilities. The Business Channel, a service of PBS/ALSS, offers specialized training and resource programming.

Libraries and museums, traditional providers of intellectual and cultural offerings, have also grown large and "cutting edge." For example, Six leading educational institutions, including Columbia University and the London School of Economics and Political Science, have formed a new site—called Fathom—to include contributions from the Cambridge University Press, the British Library, the New York Public Library, and the Smithsonian Institution's National Museum of Natural History. A for-profit Internet site, Fathom has many free offerings. Others can be accessed for a fee, including the site's own college courses and cultural offerings such as a survey of endangered mammals of North America, provided by the Smithsonian; multimedia presentations of treasured objects, such as the Magna Carta; selections from Columbia University's Oral History Research Project; and a collection of over 54,000 photographic views of New York City, from the New York Public Library.

Associations of every trade and profession provide training online; the American Society of Training Directors (ASTD) and the Learning Resource Network (LERN) offer distance instruction in how to take the training courses. You'll find programs in (and from) many corporations, as well. Much of the training previously provided by U.S. higher education, for example, is now coming from one or more of the 1600 "corporate universities" that have been created, including subsidiaries of publishing companies as well as older corporation-connected schools like the DeVry Institutes and ITT. Internally, too, corporations are using electronic training. For instance, Metropolitan Life replaces on-site seminars with scores of video conferences originating from its offices in New York or from the computer training center. The company can thus deliver training programs to employees at multiple locations simultaneously. Employees benefit from the training; employers benefit by keeping workers close to their desks.

Training programs come from all sources. Among them are the federal government and military agencies, as well as corporate Web sites of high-tech manufacturers, used for training their customers as well as their salespeople.

Fast Facts

According to the American Society for Training and Development, companies spend about $55 billion a year on formal training of all kinds. Increasingly, whether in-house or externally provided, the training is delivered electronically.

You can take college courses online, or you may find entire colleges there, including KaplanCollege.com, which bills itself as the leading provider of online professional education to help you advance your career. Some packaged programs come from places like Blackboard. At more than 3300 institutions in every state and more than 70 countries, students, teachers, and administrators are collaborating in online teaching and learning environments powered by this company's expertise and guidance. Blackboard was developed in collaboration with faculty members of Cornell University, and there are a growing number of other such companies that help colleges customize their online programs.

Fast Facts

According to the Distance Education and Training Council (DETC), "Broadening access to instructional opportunities has been a major goal of every distance education initiative. Access to distance learning has expanded as many programs have become available to students nationwide and even internationally. Originally conceived as a substitute form of education, instruction by distance education has developed into a preferred alternative for millions of people who seek education and training. Distance education programs are being offered today by colleges and universities, major corporations, large corporations and small businesses, educational agencies, government agencies, branches of the armed services, trade associations, religious institutions, service industries, political entities, private entrepreneurs and charitable, nonprofit organizations."

We're accustomed to thinking of educational providers as non-profit, even high-minded, enterprises. We can no longer assume that. Not only do many nonprofit institutions have for-profit arms, but many large educational organizations have developed with profit as an up-front motive. An example is Phoenix University, which hit the educational scene in the 1990s with something of a splash. Its president responded to a questionnaire item regarding the goals of online educational offerings this way:

> "The University of Phoenix . . . began its Online program in 1989 and today has an Online enrollment of 13,000 FTE [full-time enrolled] students . . . Yes, it has achieved the goals originally set for it but, in so doing, we have set other goals that can only be achieved by expanding the program. Consequently, *University of Phoenix Online will be spun off as a Tracking Stock. The S-3 for University of Phoenix Online was filed with the SEC [Securities and Exchange Commission] in March and we anticipate an IPO [initial public offering] in early May. With the additional resources an IPO will make available, it is our intention to increase the rate of growth from 40 percent per annum to 60 percent per annum and to undertake an aggressive international marketing campaign."* [Italics added.]

Increasingly, and increasingly openly, education is a business. Other types of commercial or for-profit providers, sometimes affiliated with universities and sometimes not, are burgeoning like mushrooms in the spring. The huge and growing numbers of providers in themselves lead to the emergence of other issues related to credentials, as online colleges offer courses that may or may not carry the credit weight you may need. Where are all those providers? You'll find lists in directories, of course—but you'd be better off checking the online sources in Appendix D for up-to-the-second references. It's not just quality, honesty, or reliability that matters to distance education enrollees, as it would to any customer of online products. With education, there are other potential glitches: certifications and credentialing questions make choosing very tough. Deciding how to begin to select from among all the providers is tough, too. We'll start that process in the next section.

Voice of Experience

Were you prepared as student or teacher?

I was new at coming back to school (after 35 years). In my very first class, the teacher announced she would be posting the homework on the computer. WHAT? I don't know how to use a computer! In my second class, the teacher announced a room change via computer. You can guess my confusion. I repeat, I had a steep learning curve for the first few weeks, but I am on the Dean's List and should be graduating with honors, basically BECAUSE of online courses.

Did you specifically seek an online course?

Yes.

How did you decide what course or program to sign on for?

Convenience—anything online is geographically desirable.

The preceding overviews of the technology, the systems, and the types of providers should give you enough background to move to the questions that are in the forefront of your choosing for success.

Is your head spinning? No wonder people describe this information stream as *buzz*. The brief introduction to the brave new world of learning offered here should convince you of the need to keep a clear head to take a sharp look at what all this means for you. The first set of questions helps you focus on whether distance learning is for you.

Part 3

Is Distance Learning for You?

Now that you've seen how many different types of distance learning there are, and how many kinds of providers offer them, you're likely becoming more convinced that you could indeed achieve success as a distance learner. This section offers a more detailed reality check with guidelines you can put to use in your own educational career.

- *The first step is to discover whether what you want to learn is offered through distributed learning.*

- *Next, be clear about why you want to study at a distance.*

- *Then, find out for yourself, before you enroll, whether you're going to be any good at this game.*

The first two chapters in this section guide you through those steps. Then, you'll have a chance to organize your own decision, with the help of other students who can help you plan your optimal course.

Chapter 5
What's in Line for Me?

What can you study effectively online? That question breaks into four parts:

1. What can be studied at a distance?
2. What do you want to study?
3. Is distance learning effective?
4. Why do you want to study at a distance?

What can be studied at a distance?

When we ask the experts what subjects can or can't be taught online or at a distance, the consistent answer is: anything can be taught—and learned—at a distance. That answer might be a bit overenthusiastic and needs a bit of hedging, as you'll find in the following text. But this list of topics taught online through courses accredited by the Distance Education and Training Council indicates the scope—and it's only a partial list. (Note that it begins with academic programs—and virtually any academic subject can be studied online, in whole or in part, for credit or not. The only exceptions, in general, are lab courses or other courses that require internships or other practical experience.)

A	Air conditioning
Academic degrees	Air force career specialties
Accident investigation	Airline/travel career training
Accounting	Air warfare
Administrative secretary	Allied health
Advertising	Animal care specialist

Appliance servicing

Army career specialties

Art composition and fundamentals

Artificial intelligence

Audio electronics

Auto detailing

Automation

Automotive electronics

Automotive mechanics

Automotive repair technician

Automotive technology

B

Banking and finance

Bartending

Beauty salon management

Bible studies

Biology

Blind, courses for

Blueprint reading

Boat design

Bookkeeping

Braille

Breastfeeding counselor

Bridal consulting

Broadcast engineering

Broadcasting radio and TV

Business administration

Business management

Business studies

Business writing

C

Career planning

Carpentry

Car rental

Cartooning

Catering

Chemistry

Child care

Children's literature

Civics

Civil engineering technology

Clerical

Coast guard career specialties

College-level subjects

College preparation

Colored stones

Color theory

Color TV technology

Commercial driver's license preparation

Commercial real estate finance

Communications

Communications technology

Computer applications

Computerized secretary

Computer literacy

Computer maintenance and repair

Computer networks

Computer programming

Computer repair technician

Computer support specialist

Computer technology
Conservation
Contracting
Cooking gourmet
Cost accounting
Counter sketching
Court reporting
Criminal justice
Cruise lines

D
Day care management
Deaf-blind home teaching preschool children
Deaf home teaching preschool children
Dental assisting
Dental office assisting/ receptionist
Design in art
Desktop publishing
Diamonds
Diamontology
Digital electronics
Doll repair
Drafting
Drafting with AutoCAD
Drawing
Dressmaking
Drywall installing and finishing

E
Early childhood education

Economics
Education
EKG technology
Electrical engineering technology
Electrician
Electricity
Electroencephalographic technology
Electronics
Elementary school courses
Engineering
Engineering design
Engines and engine tune-up
English
Enterprise development
Estate management
Executive management

F
Fashion, introduction to
Fashion merchandising
FCC general radiotelephone
FCC license preparation
Finance
Financial management
Financial planning
Firearms
Fish and wildlife management
Fitness and nutrition
Floral design
Flower arrangement and floristry

Food preparation
Food service administration
Foreign policy
Forensic science
Forestry
Freelance writing
French
Front-line management
Furniture/cabinet making

G
Gardening
GED preparation
Gem identification
Gemology
Genealogy
Geography
Gold and precious metals
Gun repair/gunsmithing

H
Health
Health care
Health care accreditation
Health care management
Health science
Heating and air conditioning
High school subjects
History
Home-based travel agents
Home health aide
Home inspection
Home living

Home remodeling and repair
Hospitality career training
Hospitality management
Hotel-motel career training
Hotel operations
Human relations
Human resource management
Hypnotherapy

I
Illustration
Income tax
Industrial electronics
Industrial engineering
  technology
Infants and toddlers with
  special needs
Information technology
Instrumentation
Insurance replacement appraisal
Intelligence studies
Interior decorating
Internal combustion engines
Internet Web page design
Introductory metrics
Investigation, criminal
Investigator

J
Java programming
Jewelry design and retailing
Jewelry display
Jewelry repair
Jewelry sales

Journalism
Junior high school subjects
Juris doctorate

K
Kindergarten

L
Lactation consultant
Landscaping
Landscaping design
Land warfare
Language, biblical
Language, foreign
Latin
Law, business
Law enforcement
Law, hotel and motel
Law, medical staff
Lawyer's assistant
Leisure and corporate agency
  training
Legal assistant
Legal nurse consulting
Legal secretary
Legal transcriptionist
Life management
Literature
Locksmithing

M
Management
Management, small business
Marine corps career specialties

Marine craft technology
Marketing
Marketing, hotel and motel
Masonry
Mathematics
Mechanics, automotive
Mechanics, diesel
Mechanics, motorcycle
Medical assisting
Medical billing
Medical coding
Medical ethics
Medical insurance clerk
Medical office assisting/
  receptionist
Medical office computer
  specialist
Medical records technology
Medical staff law
Medical staff office admini-
  stration
Medical staff organization
Medical terminology
Medical transcription
Meeting planning
Merchandising
Microcomputer repair and
  service
Microcomputers
Microprocessors
Military history
Military science
Military skills

Military studies
Modeling
Mortgage banking
Motel operations
Motorcycle repair
Motor truck sales
Motor tune-up
Multimedia
Music
Music Appreciation

N
Naval warfare
Networking
Nutrition

O
Occupational therapy aide
Oceanography
Oil Painting

P
Paralegal
Pastoral ministries
PC repair
Pearl and bead stringing
Pearls
Personnel management
Pet grooming
Pet shop assistant
Pharmacy technician
Philosophy
Photography
Physical fitness

Physical therapy
Physical therapy aide
Plumbing
Political science
Prehospital medicine
Preschool
Private investigation
Professional military education
Project management
Property management
Psychology
Public administration
Public management

Q
Quality management

R
Radar
Radio
Refrigeration
Real estate and finance
Real estate appraisal
Religion
Residential lending
Respiratory therapist
Restaurant management
Retailing
Robotics

S
Salesmanship
Science
Scoping

Secretarial

Sewing

Sheet metal

Shorthand

Small craft design

Small engine repair

Social studies

Sociology

Soldering

Sound technician

Spanish

Spanish courses written in
   Spanish language

Special needs for infants and
   toddlers

Spirituality

Stenotype machine shorthand

Supervisory development

Surveying

T

Tax procedures

Teacher's aide

Telecommunications

Television

Theology

Tourism

Training and development

Transpersonal studies

Travel agency training

Travel career training

Travel counseling

Truck driving

Truck maintenance and repair

Truck selection training

Typing

U

Unconventional warfare

Unix

U.S. history

V

VCR repair

Ventilation

Vocational electives

W

Wildlife management

World history

Writing

Y

Yacht design

If the courses you need to take involve lab work and practicums like internships or hands-on supervised work, you'll need to show up at a nonvirtual site. (You can't—yet—get a medical degree online for this very reason, but medical subjects are taught.) Likewise, most distance students still have to show up physically for exams.

What do you want to study?

In choosing what's best to learn at a distance, it turns out that this is a more important question to answer.

Fast Facts

The three most common subject areas for distance learning are business, social sciences, and education. Computer science and allied health are close seconds.

One characteristic of successful online students on which every-one—students, teachers, and researchers—seems to agree is that they have clear goals. Here, *goals* may mean long-term career aims or short-term efforts to receive specific certificates. Whatever the goals, they help keep distance students on track.

Voice of Experience

Did you specifically seek an online course?

Yes. I live an hour's drive from the nearest university which offers the courses I needed. . . . In addition, I had some specific criteria that had to be met. My goals were to be able to sit for the CPA exams in Alaska. I wanted something accredited so it would be recognized by the state. I wanted a fast program, because I've been in post-secondary education for almost seven years now. In addition, if possible, I wanted a second bachelor's degree. UMUC could help me meet all those goals.

If you aren't clear about your goals, it's best to stop now and clarify them. How? The really good learning sites offer counseling and advisement as part of their preregistration and ongoing service. Or, the educational institution sponsoring your online site should have advisers. Now's the time to seek them out. You should be able to find the counseling you need; however, if for some reason you can't find it on your real or cybercampus, you might want to check out the Web sites in Appendix D.

It's particularly important to feel ready to study online. The dropout rate in online programs is high—and one of the several reasons seems to be the lack of clarity and commitment in the students.

Fast Facts

Dropout rates in distance learning tend to be as much as 20 percent higher than for traditional courses, although there is significant variation among institutions. Some report course completion rates of more than 80 percent; others find that fewer than 50 percent of distance education students finish their courses. Comparing among institutions is misleading, however, since different schools measure retention rates differently. Some institutions, for instance, don't include in their dropout calculations those students who leave classes during drop/add periods at the beginning of a semester, while others do. Trying out an online program for a class or two is a good way to see if you're going to stick it out.

Test yourself

How do you set—or clarify—your goals? The most effective goals are SMART—that is, they are specific, meaningful, affordable, reasonable, and time-framed. For example, "I want to go back to school" is a much less effective goal than "I want to return to school to receive my BA degree in management (specific), because that will make me feel better about myself and help me achieve career advancement (meaningful). By going part-time I won't need to take out a loan (affordable). Since I'm working I will go part-time and at a distance (reasonable), and I plan to complete my studies within three years (time-framed)." See how that kind of goal setting can motivate you? It provides a matrix within which to plan your studies. Try it yourself. Even if you feel fairly clear about your purpose in education, you'll find that this exercise brings benefit—and maybe even a surprise. The following self-test may point you toward effective study goals.

Answers to questions like these will help keep your goals up front as you investigate and ask questions about distance learning courses—and later as you become immersed in the work itself.

		Specific	Meaningful	Affordable	Reasonable	Time-framed
I am studying	WHAT					
	WHY					
	HOW					
	WHERE					
	WHEN					

Sum up your goals in a personal statement: _____

(For example: "I am studying to receive a degree in _____ so that I can change careers to _____ . I'll be able to use my computer and can afford to take two courses at a time, so that I can finish my program by three years from now.")

With goals like this in mind, it becomes easier to choose the course of study that is best for you—and, given the fact that almost anything can be studied effectively, that personal viewpoint is what will make the difference between success and disappointment. So, when you're looking at what's best to study online, the first answer is: whatever subject you feel strongest about.

Does it work?

Based on a fairly large amount of research, you can safely operate from the assumption that you're as likely to have a successful educational experience with a distance course as with a more traditional variety.

In Other Words

The consensus is that distance education is effective. Experts comment that research comparing distance education with traditional face-to-face instruction indicates that teaching and studying at a distance can be as effective as traditional instruction when the method and technologies used are appropriate to the instructional tasks, when there is interaction among students, and when there is timely teacher-to-student feedback.

Is distance learning effective?

According to the U.S. government, preliminary findings from a number of studies have been quite positive. The U.S. Office of Technology Assessment, sponsored by Congress, has found in several reports that distance learners do as well as or better than traditional students in their courses and on achievement tests. For example, when the same graduate-level course was taught simultaneously at two traditional campuses (Georgia Tech and the University of Alabama) and one online school (National Technical University), it was found that distance students not only learned more but also gained social skills and a network of student peers. And annual comparisons done by the University of Phoenix have consistently found that distance students perform as well as or better than their campus-based peers in their classes, and interact with the instructor and each other more. So you can assume that distance learning can be just as effective as traditional classroom activities, if not more so.

In Other Words

Five Guiding Principles for Distance Learning, adapted from the American Council on Education

- There is no one best instructional delivery and interaction media or method. Media and methods are selected for their contribution to the achievement of the learning outcome in a given situation.

- A true learning community is interactive where participants have the opportunity to engage information, their teacher and their fellow students.

- All learning environments, traditional and virtual, are important to the university and will be cared for.

- A systems approach to instructional design will be modeled.

- Technology is a tool that enables distance and distributed learning to occur.

Why do you want to study at a distance?

If the following are any of your reasons:

- *"It's faster."*
- *"It's cheaper."*
- *"It's easier."*
- *"It means I don't have to deal with other people."*

then distance learning is not for you, because, as we've noted, distance education is neither faster, cheaper, easier, nor less socially involved.

But, if your reasons are to:

- *Fit learning into your schedule of family and job demands*
- *Keep education consistent despite a move or major change*
- *Get a good education when a campus is hours away*
- *Make a start on returning to school when you're feeling timid about joining a class*

then distance learning is a good move.

Here's what people have to say about their experiences:

> I raised three sons and helped put my husband through college before I began to think about my own education. As a full-time real estate broker, I knew I wouldn't be able to pursue a bachelor's degree in a traditional format. After reading an article about cyberlearning, I decided to do some research on the possibility of learning via the Internet.
>
> I wanted to be able to earn a degree in a format that would allow a flexible schedule. In my case, traveling up to the campus would take about an hour each direction. Most courses were offered in the daytime, and the evening courses were limited, and due to prerequisites, the pro-

gram of study could take many years to complete, as not all programs were offered at night.

After working all day, this would mean commuting to the school, during rush hour, several nights a week. In many cases, I could do the course work in the DL [distance learning] format in less time than the commute to the live course would take! Also, we have all sat through a late evening course where everyone, including the instructor, was tired and didn't really want to be there! With DL I could watch the lectures and do the assignments when it suited my schedule best.

On the other hand, the very busyness of these students' lives can actually lead to disappointment in online study. As one experienced and successful online instructor observes, "I think the type of student who takes an online class is one that is trying really hard, but sometimes gets in over his head." One important step toward online success might be to start with one course or with a noncredit class to see what it's really like for you.

Online learning has some benefits that classroom learning may lack, however. The online environment requires the learner to be actively involved in his or her own learning and provides both a series of choices to make and an immediate response to each action, so participation demands more, engages more, and empowers more than the traditional approaches.

In sum, we could say that just as distance, online, and asynchronous learning have made the educational process more student centered, so the effectiveness of what's offered depends on the students themselves. Anything can be taught; it's just a matter of the student being engaged. And, to an unprecedented extent, choice is in the student's hands, too—that's next.

Chapter 6

Success Scan

Does your schedule change from day to day?

> Do you want to keep learning—but not to sit in a chair from 5:30 to 9:30 P.M. every Tuesday and Thursday evening?

Are you too busy for traditional education?

> Parents, caregivers, working adults—and anyone who needs flexibility—may find distance learning to be the best way to combine studies and life.

All this makes distance learning sound so appealing, doesn't it? But is there anyone who shouldn't try distance education? It may be that everyone should try it at least once, so that if they choose not to get involved, they are making an educated choice and not assuming that they don't like distance learning.

However, just as some potential students assume they can't study online because they are technologically incompetent, there are others who assume that anyone will make a good online student, no matter what their approach to learning or what subjects they need to learn. "Not so," say the experts. Before spending (or wasting) time and money to join a course or program that is not right for you, you'll be better off knowing ahead of time what you should be doing, because one aspect of online learning that the hype hides is the particularly high dropout rate from online classes—much higher than for other types of courses. To an extent, this can be blamed on frustration with technical glitches or teachers who lack online skills. But at least as often, it's on the student's part: the discomfort with technology, with isolation, or with distance, or the absence of a clear study goal.

These are all factors you can find out for yourself, and it's worth the time to do so. You'll have a better chance of sticking with your education plan if you check yourself out before you check into class. Are distance learning courses right for you? They might be, if:

- *You have a full-time job (or two) on a schedule that precludes class attendance*
- *You live some distance from class*
- *Your family responsibilities make scheduling a class difficult*
- *You have clear goals and a determination to reach them*

You can become completely clear about your suitability by taking some simple self-tests. Many sites have self-tests that cover most of the following areas:

Your skills
Your goals
Your attitudes
Your abilities

In fact, finding such a self-eliminating test is a sign of a valuable site—because it's a sign that the institution cares more about you than about itself. In this chapter, you'll find some self-profiling tests to try.

....

Fast Facts

Profile of a "typical" online student:

Over 25

Employed

Caregiver

Some higher education

Equally likely to be male or female

....

Are you a good candidate for online learning?

Many online schools offer self-profiles you can take to determine if you're suitable. If your school doesn't, add that to the debit side of your choice list (see Chapter 7). Chances are, if you have an odd or tight schedule, live far away from campus, have many others dependent on you during "normal hours," or are interested in a program that's not offered nearby, then you're probably ready to take the next steps. Of course, it may be that you simply want to learn online. Still, you'd do well to run through these self-tests to help find a fit. In this chapter you'll find the kinds of questions that good distance learning (DL) programs ask their potential students.

For starters, use the following self-test to evaluate yourself. How many a's did you mark? The more of those answers that fit, the better suited you are to distance learning.

Self-test

1. Which statement best describes you?

   (a) I am a self-starter with solid personal motivation.

   (b) I need occasional prodding to accomplish goals.

   (c) I don't work independently and require constant prodding or reminders.

2. I learn best:

   (a) When I hear material (auditory).

   (b) When I see it (visual).

   (c) When I can both hear and see the material.

3. As a worker:

   (a) I usually meet or beat deadlines.

   (b) I have a hard time getting focused by myself.

   (c) I procrastinate to the last minute and beyond.

4. On tests and other school assignments:

   (a) I figure out instructions on my own.

   (b) I can usually follow the directions, but I like them to be available.

   (c) I have difficulty figuring out instructions on my own and need to hear them read to me.

(continued)

5. When I turn in an assignment, I like feedback from the teacher:

    (a) Within a reasonable amount of time.

    (b) Within a day or two, or I become distracted.

    (c) Immediately.

6. When it comes to the organization of the class material:

    (a) I can learn even if the class is not highly structured.

    (b) I like some structure in the class.

    (c) I feel very uncomfortable without structure.

7. Dealing with technology:

    (a) I have excellent computer skills.

    (b) I have some computer and Internet facility.

    (c) I am not very familiar with a computer and do not feel comfortable surfing the Net.

8. When I am asked to use VCRs, TVs, computers, e-mail, or other technologies:

    (a) I have little or no difficulty learning new skills.

    (b) I am glad to try and ask for help if necessary.

    (c) I frequently get frustrated and may prefer to avoid computer work.

Then use the checklist to profile yourself:

Checklist

Yes	No	
_____	_____	1. I have access to a computer and/or the multimedia equipment required for a distance learning experience.
_____	_____	2. I am not intimidated by using technology applications for learning.
_____	_____	3. I feel comfortable using a computer for basic word processing, using the Internet, and sending/receiving e-mail.
_____	_____	4. I have strong time management skills and am able to meet deadlines and keep track of assignments, and I enjoy and am successful at independent learning.
_____	_____	5. I am able to learn successfully without face-to-face interaction with others.
_____	_____	6. I can easily express my ideas, comments, and questions verbally and in writing.
_____	_____	7. I am generally flexible and can easily adjust to changing schedules.
_____	_____	8. I do have some time to go to campus for tests and meetings.
_____	_____	9. I am a self-starter.
_____	_____	10. I am a good time manager.
_____	_____	11. I am capable of self-discipline.
_____	_____	12. I am good at comprehending what I read.
_____	_____	13. I am goal-directed—if I set my sights on a result, I usually achieve it.

(continued)

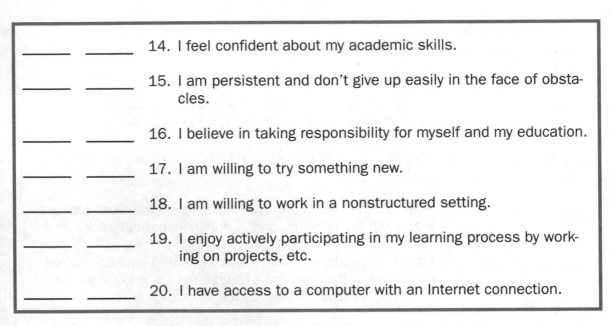

_____ _____ 14. I feel confident about my academic skills.

_____ _____ 15. I am persistent and don't give up easily in the face of obstacles.

_____ _____ 16. I believe in taking responsibility for myself and my education.

_____ _____ 17. I am willing to try something new.

_____ _____ 18. I am willing to work in a nonstructured setting.

_____ _____ 19. I enjoy actively participating in my learning process by working on projects, etc.

_____ _____ 20. I have access to a computer with an Internet connection.

If you answered yes to at least 15 of these statements, online courses may be right for you! But, if you answered yes to fewer than 15, you might want to rethink your interest in an online program.

Voice of Experience

"Not for me," says one student: "I'm not too organized, and with the online course you really have to be disciplined. You really have to schedule your time and work at home. I need to know that my class is at 5 P.M. Wednesday: that's when I have to be there, and that's when my work is due."

You also might want to look at how great your immediate need is for this course. Some students sign on at a distance because it's the only way they can take a particular course to fit their educational requirements. But some just think it would be a nifty idea. The stronger your need for the course, and the more difficult traditional attendance is, the more likely you are to succeed online. Compare these situations:

Alyson is a young mother who needs to work, who can't afford child care, and who needs a certificate to get a better job. She's arranged to work in child care (with her toddler) in the mornings; "then when she's down for a nap, I study, and when she's up she sometimes sits on my lap while I go online. At night I can write my papers." If Alyson can keep at this, she'll have a certificate in a year and a half that will give her much higher-paying work.

Bettina is also a young mother who is home with her toddlers all day and has decided that she might want to be a writer, so she's signed on for a Web-based course. She has a hard time breaking free from the kids, and somehow hadn't counted on the amount of writing time the course would require.

It's easy to see which online student is more likely to stick with it. Bettina has probably wasted the money she put into tuition.

Or, there's the business executive who's up for a job in a high-tech firm. He needs to learn a lot about the Web quickly. He's found some great courses, and even though he has to access his courses by laptop from plane flights, he's determined to take this next career step. He is much more likely to stick with his educational project than his colleague, also a busy executive, who is thinking that a career change might be a good idea and has signed on for a class on Web design with an eye toward starting his own business someday.

Motive and commitment—do you have them? When you visualize yourself going to school, do you see yourself hanging a diploma on the wall, or having coffee with your classmates at the diner after class? Just because online is in doesn't mean that you can't go to school in the old-fashioned, friend-filled manner.

Keep in mind that:

- *Distance and distributed learning situations, especially in an asynchronous environment, require the learner to be self-disciplined and motivated, to stay on task, and to complete assignments with minimal structure.*

- *While many distance and distributed learning environments may not include any face-to-face interaction between the learner and the instructor, you will find a need to interact with fellow students via e-mail and through audio and video conferencing—and a significant component of many courses is a team project or two.*

Voice of Experience

The Penn State online college—World Campus—is a thorough provider of both courses and support. It sums up the points to keep in mind:

On a technical level, World Campus students must

- be familiar with computers and the Internet. . . . A demo course walks you through the various technical skills you'll need to be successful. You'll also need to have access to a computer system that meets the minimum technical requirements.

- be able to read and write in the English language. Proficiency in English is required, and international student applicants for credit certificates and credit courses whose first language is not English should consider taking the Test of English as a Foreign Language (TOEFL).

But having technical competence alone won't make you a successful distance learner. Distance education is both an opportunity and a challenge—an opportunity to take courses in a flexible learning environment and a challenge to shape your life and direct your own studies. Distance education requires self-discipline and persistence. You will need to hone your planning skills so that you can make the best use of your study time. You'll also find that the ability to research topics effectively and efficiently will come in handy, especially in graduate-level courses. And, for courses that take advantage of collaborative learning strategies, you'll find that teamwork skills are also important to possess.

Voice of Experience

Online teachers say that the classes work because online students are "more motivated than folks who doze through classroom lectures," and "because students can't fake assignments" or "hide at the back of the class."

- *Despite the high-tech nature of distance education programs, writing skills are important, because all distance learning environments have written components. Verbal communica-*

tion ability is also important when communicating via the audio components. It is also important to read competently, as all instructions, whether in print or on-screen, are written.

- *Flexibility and adaptability are also important, as technology may require unplanned changes and reorganization may be needed fairly often.*

- *Technical skills are probably last on the list: while you'll be more comfortable accessing your course, classmates, and instructor through a variety of media, this is the aspect of distance learning that most students pick up most quickly.*

In Other Words

Educators comment that in an online environment, there are indeed classmates who form a bond and can create a kind of pacing. However, online learners are still required to have clear goals and to be reasonably self-disciplined. And it's important to keep your goals in mind, according to the Oregon Community College Distance Education Consortium. It's easy for distance learners to neglect coursework because of personal or professional circumstances—unless they have compelling reasons to stay on track.

Low-tech learning

Remember that not all distance education programs involve computers, modems, or other e-machines. As described in Chapter 2, you can take a class by TV, by tape, by mail, or at distance in-class sites. If all this computer talk seems uncomfortable, why not check out as many demo online courses as you can—then consider some of the other options that might meet your needs? One thing that all the high-tech talk makes us forget is that the new forms of delivery provide added *choices,* not added *demands,* about our education.

In sum, you're likely headed for online success if you:

1. Are comfortable managing your own schedule

2. Have a workable goal to plan toward

3. Know what you're getting into ahead of time (use the next section to learn how to apply this to specific programs)

After going through the pros and cons, facts, and comments in the past sections, take a look at where you are. Put some plans in writing here.

Goals for learning: _____

Course of study: _____

Type of provider: _____

Part 4

How to Choose a Distance Education Provider

With the distance learning basics under your belt and a sense that, indeed, there's a course or program out there for you somewhere, you're ready to make some specific choices. How to select an online program? There are now so many out there that it can be overwhelming—and, whether for a class or a degree, the choice is really all yours to make. As the *Chronicle of Higher Education* puts it, it's up to the student to "kick the tires and check the mileage," since widely accepted systems for evaluating online learning programs haven't been established.

In this section, the focus is on the key elements to examine, the process of sorting out the possibilities, and the essential information—including how to pay for this!—to gather before signing on.

Chapter 7

The Steps to Take

You'll find as much variety in the content and quality of online learning programs as in any kind of education, so it's important to be clear about what you can expect before you sign up for a program or even a class. The first step is to do—yes—some homework: search the Web for the subjects you want to study, and go online (or to the library or bookstore) to find listings and directories that describe distance learning programs. (You'll find some listed in Appendix D.)

Here's how the process might work.

1. If you know the subjects you want to study, search for them in lists like the one provided by the Distance Education and Training Council (DETC) (see Appendix D) or by using Web search engines (Yahoo!, Netscape, and the like), or both.

2. Follow up by clicking on the links to the institutions or organizations that offer courses on your subjects.

3. If you can't find your special topics—or if you're looking for programs that might be recommended for certain specializations (as, say, for nursing)—go to the sites of associations that specialize in your area of interest and contact them for guidance to courses.

4. If you're more concerned with the location or the name of the school, you can find lists of online providers at sites like those of the University Continuing Education Association (UCEA) and the DETC. You may need to study close to home if the program requires occasional on-site attendance, or your profession may only approve credentials from a certain few institutions.

5. If all you care about is the online aspect of the provider, use a search engine to explore the topic "online education."

6. However you collect the possible providers, your next step is to visit their sites. You can ask for catalogs to be sent to you, or you should be able to get all the information you need online.

Then what? Once you've taken these simple research steps, you may well find yourself face-to-face with the demon of the twenty-first century: information overload. You have loads of detailed data—and all the formats look good (or they should). But the data may not be factual, and the appealing Web site may be a thin facade. Is it a diploma mill hiding behind what seems to be a famous name? Or is it high-quality education offered by a little-known institution? It's up to you to find the quality you need.

Following the sitemap

Certain elements are—or should be—common to all distance education programs.

Fast Facts

The Center for the Study of Distance Learning summarizes:

Success in technology-based programs is based on an ability to meet educational needs; an orientation to the learner, not the teacher; cost effectiveness; a reliance on simple delivery systems; and a systems-design format. Other factors that need to be considered are the reliability of the technology, the suitability of other media, local production ability, standardization, appropriate designs and information, scheduling, and appropriate levels of human interaction.

As you explore the Web sites of each possibility, keep a lookout for some key elements. Here's what you'll need to "kick the tires." Student-friendly distance education providers offer easy-to-access information covering:

Accreditation status

Credentials of presenters

Application/registration processes

Financial and financial aid information

Listings of technical requirements

Detailed descriptions of programs and formats

Catalogs available by mail or online

Responsive advisement systems

Demonstration classes

As for checking the mileage, most modern distance education providers don't have much mileage or track records to check. In some cases, you may be able to contact alumni for information, and the site should provide statistics on enrollment figures and graduation rates. If it's too new, it may not have gotten the kinks out of its cords yet. And some virtual universities have already folded: California Virtual University, which opened with a lot of flash and was to serve as a clearinghouse for distance education programs at about 100 public colleges and universities in California, gave up after only eight months, due apparently to poor planning. Potential students need to use careful judgment, since they can't always (or even often) rely on the name of a preexisting institution to guarantee the stability of a new version of the school. Another developing trend is the commercialization of existing well-respected institutions. NYUOnline.com, for example, does *not* offer the huge range of programs of New York University; rather, it presents just a few noncredit management programs. Kick those tires!

Voice of Experience

"I researched several fields. My criteria: it had to pay, be quick to learn, and make me the last one fired. I visited several schools, took a few disappointing courses and ultimately chose a more solid university-based program. I strongly recommend visiting all training facilities and checking out the hardware. My first unfortunate choice was short on instructor skills and riddled with hardware problems, making it difficult to see where the mistakes occurred—me or the system."

You'll want to look for other positive characteristics, like:

- *All-encompassing programs that provide access to learning materials as well as on-site information, backed by resources like an online academic research library, direct access to regional library networks, or both.*

- *Thoroughly planned, carefully tested, and easy access to these learning resources.*

- *More focus on the content and quality of the courses offered and the students served than on the technology: educational theorists stress the importance of a focus on instructional outcomes, noting that technology should serve content, not vice versa.*

Voice of Experience

Teacher Judy Smith says, "I've been teaching online for about seven years, primarily for universities with well-developed online programs. When I say well-developed, I mean a specific 'platform' for course delivery was in place at the time. The institutions were not trying to 'come up with something' on their own, without the benefit of programmers and educational technologists to contribute to the discussion. I think this made a difference in the fact that these same institutions are still in business, and growing every day. The platforms they have are successful, scalable, and constantly under thorough review. A good platform that resists crashes, is easy to use, and provides direct access to a faculty member or facilitator is absolutely key. If the technology and platform are perceived to be 'clunky' or disorganized, the adult learner will *not* use the product."

Issues alert

As new providers—and entirely new forms—of learning are rapidly coming to a boil, some significant issues are bubbling up. As a background for making your education decision, you'd be wise to be aware of some of the following, as highlighted by recent headlines from the *Chronicle of Higher Education*.

Accreditation

So far, there is no standard accreditation for online programs, as noted in these headlines:

> Assessing the Quality of Online Courses Remains a Challenge, Educators Agree (2/18/2000)
>
> Education Dept. and Career Schools Clash Over Accrediting of Distance Learning (12/17/99)
>
> 'Virtual' Institutions Challenge Accreditors to Devise New Ways of Measuring Quality (8/6/99)
>
> Role of Accreditors in Distance Education Is Debated at Conference (2/12/99)

Relationship to academic institutions

In most cases, academe doesn't quite know how to relate to new forms of education—and in only a few cases are the old-line institutions moving fast enough to keep up with the newer providers. For example:

> Law Professors Told to Expect Competition From Virtual Learning (1/21/2000)
>
> Historians Differ on Impact of Distance Education in Their Discipline (1/21/2000)
>
> Faculty Report at U. of Illinois Casts Skeptical Eye on Distance Education (1/14/2000)
>
> Students' F's Highlight Problems in Electronic Course at U. of Iowa (11/26/99)
>
> Mount Holyoke Looks at How the Web Can Improve Classroom Instruction (4/7/2000)
>
> Even Public Speaking Can Be Taught Online (3/24/2000)
>
> Online Psychology Instruction Is Effective, but Not Satisfying, Study Finds (3/10/2000)
>
> Indiana U. Scholar Says Distance Education Requires New Approach to Teaching (3/10/2000)

Regulation and quality control

In Some States, Governors Are Told, Distance Learning Is Too Regulated (3/10/2000)

A Key Senator Dismisses Need for Legislation to Assure the Quality of Distance Education (2/18/2000)

Kansas Sues the Owner of an On-Line University That Allegedly Sold Degrees (8/20/99)

Louisiana Tries to Close Loopholes That Allow Suspected Diploma Mills to Thrive (5/14/99)

The Bubble Bursts for Education Dot-Coms (6/30/00)

All of these headline issues come together in two factors that could directly impact you as a potential student: quality and honesty. The often conflicting relationship of the academy to the Web site of a given institution can create confusion for the consumer, since conflict between who's offering what sometimes results in Web offerings that are misleading. More serious for all concerned are the outright scams—the so-called diploma mills, which sell worthless credentials for a fee—and worse, the totally phony sites that just take your money.

In Other Words

The *Chronicle of Higher Education* also reports: "With a glut of online-education providers springing into the academic world, students may have trouble distinguishing the good from the bad." And experts offer little comfort: they say that as students surf the Web for online courses, it's up to them to make sure they get a quality education.

Some examples: recent news reports describe what experts called the biggest—though certainly not the only—diploma scam to hit the Internet. By e-mail, it promised an online "degree" for as little as $500. "No one is turned down" by this phony university—and no one need attend class or turn in papers, either. The operation has actually gone on for quite a while, using a variety of names—the most recent being Harrington University. Diploma mills have been around for decades, but now that the wide reach of the Internet can rake in even more cash for worthless pieces of paper, they are entering a boom stage again—and they are very hard to track down. For $1500, a purchaser can get a fictitious diploma, which costs the provider almost nothing.

Another kind of almost-scam takes the opposite tack: "free" courses. Education has become one of the hottest marketing tools for Web sites. By offering free classes, they also have the opportunity to gather information about you as you click through the site. One new Web site offers free courses—with regular interactive ads. Founders of a new Web site called FreeEdu offer more than 600 minicourses free. The catch: users have to answer questionnaires about commercial products on a regular basis. Instead of charging students tuition or placing banner advertisements throughout the site, FreeEdu generates revenue through deals with companies that will pay to poll students about their knowledge of various products and services. The surveys pop up once every 30 minutes, and the actual content of the (noncredit) course is of variable quality. Is this education? Your choice.

Luckily, there *is* quality education online to choose from. For example, the Institute for Higher Education Policy has studied quality distance education programs. The study established benchmarks for quality distance education by exploring best practices at six experienced distance higher education providers—Brevard Community College, Cocoa, Florida; Regents College, Albany, New York; the University of Illinois at Urbana-Champaign, the University of Maryland University College, College Park, Maryland; Utah State University, Logan, Utah; and Weber State University, Ogden, Utah— and drew conclusions about common benchmarks of quality, which included solid technical platforms, a focus on the student, and quality content. An examination of the sites of these providers can offer a baseline for comparison as you explore all the providers on the net.

There is bad news and good news. The bad news is that you have to be extremely careful in considering an educational provider these days. The good news? Given all the choices, it's possible to make an excellent selection—and the power to choose is with the student. Academics and other educators have noted that modern education is, almost suddenly, student-driven. As the student or potential student, you do the selecting.

How am I going to pay for it?

As you explore, you may find that one piece of information isn't so easy to uncover: "how much will this cost?" The answer depends on the program (more on this in the next chapter). And though most Americans have come to accept that education can be expensive, what may come as a surprise is that not only is online or other distance learning *not* less expensive than traditional varieties, but it can be harder to pay for. If the class you sign on to is one part of your wider higher education enrollment, it's (most likely) included in the bill covered by your financial aid package. But if your program is primarily online or distance learning, it is likely not to be covered by financial aid.

Here's why: students who take classes online have been shut out from financial aid in part because the federal Higher Education Act makes students ineligible for aid if their college enrolls more than 50 percent of its students—or offers more than 50 percent of its courses—via distance education. Another financial aid rule holds that the academic year must be at least 30 weeks long for a student to get the maximum amount of financial aid.

Many of these rules were imposed to protect students against fraud by so-called correspondence schools. Pilot projects are under way to study new rules, and legislative efforts are under way to try to change them—but in the meantime, what do you do? First, focus on courses that are on a term basis—with a clear beginning and end date. Such courses are covered by federal aid. The difference comes when courses are on "rolling enrollment." One of the advantages of many distance learning programs is their "anywhere/anytime" quality—but, if you can't afford to pay the bills for those, go for the more standard schedules. Affordability can be one key factor in helping you to choose between one course and another.

If you're a matriculated, full-time student at an institution for which distance education systems provide part of the education, all the financial aid information you'll find from the standard sources applies for distance programs as well. For less traditional programs, you will find financial support. There are Pell grants for part-time learners, for instance, and special funding for minority groups or others with special characteristics. There's also the G.I. Bill and the Defense Activity for Non-Traditional Education Support (DANTES) program, a tuition program for military service members. Find out about all of them from sites like the Student Financial Assistance Programs Web site, at http://www.ed.gov/offices/OSFAP/Students/. Among the many useful items here, you will find the Free Application for Federal Student Aid (FAFSA). Use it to apply for federal financial aid and for many state student aid programs. Electronic versions of the FAFSA make applying for financial aid faster and easier than ever.

The government site also contains the Student Guide to Financial Aid, the Directory of State Guaranty Agencies and State Grant Agencies, and the HOPE Scholarships and Lifetime Learning Tax Credits site, which provides helpful guidance on how to obtain tax benefits (including relevant IRS notices) for adults returning to school and for parents sending their children to college.

For College cost information, check College Opportunities On-Line (COOL), developed by the National Center for Education Statistics. This site presents data on college prices and information on financial aid, enrollment, and types of programs that are offered. The COOL searchable database is designed to help students, future students, and their parents understand the differences between colleges and how much it costs to attend college.

The Student Guide to Financial Aid is the most comprehensive resource on student financial aid from the U.S. Department of Education. Grants, loans, and work study are the three major forms of student financial aid available through the federal Student Financial Assistance Programs. Updated each award year, the Student Guide tells you about the programs and how to apply for them.

You may also be eligible for tax cuts for education, and you can find out about these at the federal aid site. For information on direct loans, there's a loan Web site link—and a gateway to government link that will help you explore all the opportunities in the federal government. Access America provides links to recognized accrediting agencies as well. If a postsecondary school offers federal student aid, it is probably accredited by one of these agencies.

Fast Facts

Federal money is available for nontraditional study from the following sources:

Federal Pell Grants

Federal Supplemental Educational Opportunity Grants

Federal Work Study

Federal Perkins Loans

Federal Stafford Loans

Federal PLUS Loans

HOPE Fellowships

Tax Benefits for Higher Education

Under IRS rules, you may withdraw funds from an individual retirement account (IRA) without penalty for your own higher education expenses or those of your spouse, child, or even grandchild. (But check with the IRS or an accountant to confirm that this is still in effect before taking action!) The HOPE and lifetime learning tax credits can reduce your tax bill if you're paying for your own or your dependent's college education. All of this is worth looking into before you make your final education plans.

Fast Facts

UCEA partners with Sallie Mae to offer Career Training Loan Program

The University Continuing Education Association joins with SLM Financial Corporation, a subsidiary of Sallie Mae, to promote the Career Training Loan Program. As part of this initiative, SLM is also joining UCEA as a corporate sponsor. The Career Training Loan Program makes low-interest education loans available to continuing and distance education students at UCEA member institutions, regardless of whether they are enrolled on a full- or part-time basis. Participating students will benefit from rates as low as prime + 1 percent, 24-hour loan approval (more than 70 percent of applications are approved), the ability to borrow the entire cost of their tuition and qualifying expenses, and up to 15 years to repay with no prepayment penalty. UCEA, an association of nontraditional education providers, is at www.nucea.edu.

Quality, reliability, and finance are all big issues (and ones you'll rarely notice in the promotional flyers for your dot-com learning!). But, step by step, you gather your possibilities, you compare prices and offerings, you check out the demo classes. You narrow your search to the most likely possibilities. The next chapter shows how to make the final cut: simply ask the right questions!

Chapter 8

What to Look For

When you've gathered all the available information, you'll discover that even similar education institutions have widely varying definitions of distance learning. Some offer TV programs or even videos as a distance education program, while others can connect you to sophisticated systems through which you can gain highly technical expertise. In between are the online programs that the majority of virtual students are becoming accustomed to, which connect them to an instructor via a personal computer. Even there, you'll find a wide variation. So, just as you would when you're shopping for any service, you'll need to ask questions to be sure to get the format that's best for you.

You may ask these questions in person if you're applying to a college, or you might ask them on-line or by e-mail. This is not to say that you must have a computer before you sign up for online courses (though over 150 million Americans have Internet access). You will need equipment and some computer skills—but some schools offer computers for connection to their courses, especially (but not only) to on-campus students.

Answers to get

More important than getting information on the equipment and the technology, though, is being clear about the program you're signing on to. Here are some questions to ask when considering an online course:

- *Is it accredited?*
  - ★ *What organization accredits it?*
  - ★ *Is its accreditation part of that of the larger institution?*

- *Can I apply, enroll, and pay online, or will I need an in-person interview?*

- *Is the entire course online? Will I need to attend class? Where?*

  ★ *Exactly how is the learning distributed?*

  ★ *Can I do assignments from home or must I go on-site?*

- *Is the online program independent, or is it a part of a more traditional study format?*

  ★ *Will I need to enroll in a full-fledged degree program?*

  ★ *Can I incorporate the online courses into study from other schools?*

- *Can I see a sample of the courses?*

  ★ *Do you have a demo?*

  ★ *May I sit in?*

- *What is the class structure?*

  ★ *Are sessions synchronous or asynchronous?*

  ★ *Do you use chat rooms? E-mail? Other?*

- *What equipment is needed?*

  ★ *Can I use just a standard personal computer (PC) with modem?*

  ★ *Will I need an Integrated Services Digital Network (ISDN) line?*

  ★ *Do you provide equipment? Software?*

Fast Facts

In the absence of third-party ratings, making contact with a student or alumnus of an online program would seem to be a sensible step to take in evaluating such a program—but the situation may not be so simple. Privacy laws restrict institutions from giving out information about students or graduates. If someone chats on a forum, posts on a bulletin board you can access, or gives permission to be contacted, you can't reach them. Note that some sites quote "satisfied customers," but these people have of course been cleared by the providers of the site and so may not be offering an objective view. It may be possible to find alumni listed in alumni publications, though, so that could be worth a try.

....

- *What kind of technical assistance do you offer?*
  - ★ *Is it accessible 24 hours a day?*
  - ★ *Do you offer initial training?*
- *What subject matter do you offer?*
  - ★ *Are these the same courses offered by the rest of the institution?*
- *If certification is offered, is it a credential that will be accepted in my home state?*
- *Is course content strictly canned, or is there actual interaction possible, such as virtual snack bars for socializing and study groups for support?*
- *For name institutions: who is providing the curriculum— your faculty or some other supplier?*
- *For new institutions: who are you? How long have you been providing courses? Who teaches the classes?*
- *How much does your program cost?*
  - ★ *What does that include?*
  - ★ *Does it include costs of software, hardware, and connectors?*
  - ★ *Can I get any kind of financial aid?*

But don't just ask the provider. Ask:

- *The Department of Education in the state where the school is located.*
- *The licensing or certification agencies that cover your job and job training.*

- *The Better Business Bureau nearest the university in question.*

- *Your gut: if your instincts say there's more flash than substance, listen to them!*

And remember that you can check all accreditation claims with the U.S. Department of Education, or with agencies listed in Appendix D.

On a more personal level, you'll want to know about what you'll actually experience in class, including:

- *How do students communicate with each other? Do they ever meet? When?*

- *How do students communicate with the professor? How often are students contacted?*

- *Can I contact any of the students or alumni?*

- *How often will I need to participate in the class? Write papers? Take tests?*

- *Are the faculty members comfortable working with adult learners?*

- *How responsive are the instructors?*

Seek solid clues

Don't just ask: look for clues to a solid program. While you will want to visit many educational sites before choosing a program, you'll want to judge more than the cover of the site and really get inside. Anyone can design an attractive Web site, but the site is only the facade for the content and function. You wouldn't choose a college by standing on its campus and looking at the fronts of the buildings—likewise, you'll really want to explore the sites you're focusing on.

It's not even enough to find what appears to be a student-friendly site—though demo classes, self-tests, and other outreach devices are important. You need to go beyond these features. Is the site easy to navigate? Does it allow you to move around smoothly, or does it seem overly wrapped up with its own coolness? Does it provide answers to all the questions you might have? Does it list information (phone numbers, addresses, fax numbers) for making low-tech contact with the provider? Does it fully list everything it offers? These factors can be clues to programs that have been put together with some thought. Find out what you can about the administering of the program:

- *Its planning: is it for the benefit of the student or of the institution?*

- *Its equipment: is it reliable?*

- *Its help system: is there easy access to skilled technical support?*

- *Its instructional design: will it teach what it says it will teach?*

- *Its instructor training: are the teachers comfortable with the system?*

- *Its administrative support: is the school geared to deal with distance learners?*

- *Its support services: are the bookstore, library, and instructors easily available?*

Check it Out

Those who've been there say a lot of the criteria are based on common sense:

Do you find traditional quality indicators?

Good reputation

Longevity

Good student-teacher ratio

Does it meet your goals?

To learn a specific task or skill

To get a credential

To get a job

For a skill, almost any site will do. To get a credential, you'll want an accredited or at least professionally approved provider. To get a job, it's better to go to a better-known school,

Take a tour!

Visit the sites and do the demos. Find out firsthand what kind of orientation is offered. (If it's not offered at the sample site, you can be pretty sure it won't be there for you when you're a student!) Look for tech support in the form of:

- *Web pages*

- *An online database of technical answers*

- *Online training courses and reference materials*

- *An online help desk where you can easily communicate your computer problem and get the assistance you need—as well as live support*

Voice of Experience

The Center for the Study of Distance Learning lists as keys to successful programs evidence of a provider's skill at:

- Planning for technology

- Using reliable equipment

- Offering easy access to technical support

- Instructional design that is both educationally effective and easy to access

- Instructor training for effective teaching and management of technology

- Providing learner support services such as registration, advising, and office hours

As an outsider to the process of developing educational programs, you can have no direct knowledge of what's behind what you see on your screen or in the catalog. Some providers are offering an educational product for the primary purpose of making money (or luring you into a site where they will make money). Others, with loftier goals, may not be competent at putting a program out there. In either case, you may be shelling out cash with no solid instructional return. In seeking quality, the Distance Education and Training Council (DETC) looks for good management/administrative support—"top-down support for distance learning"—to ensure effective strategies for program development and promotion, and instructional development, as well as funding support." Signs of that kind of backup support will show in the quality and depth of a site.

Some other approaches: ask potential employers about what they think of training or education provided by the sites you're considering. You can also contact the Better Business Bureau and the Department of Education in the area where your provider's headquarters are.

When quality counts

This kind of indirect evaluation may be all you can hope for, since systems for rating online and other distance programs are not in wide use. Courses and programs that are offered as part of a wider curriculum of a college or university are in most cases covered by the institution's accreditation. Other programs are accredited by various groups (for example, associations that may sponsor training programs), such as the DETC, which is a government-approved group, or the Instructional Technology Consortium (ITC), a national non-profit organization that represents postsecondary educational institutions that are involved in distance learning.

Fast Facts

Accreditation bodies need accreditation themselves!

The two entities that recognize accrediting agencies in the United States are the U.S. Department of Education and the Council for

Higher Education Accreditation (CHEA). CHEA publishes an annual directory, *Accredited Institutions of Postsecondary Education.*

In addition to exploring for yourself, or looking for providers that are accredited, you can ask the evaluators your own questions, such as:

If I get a high school diploma from a DETC-accredited institution, will I be accepted into a college or university?

DETC answer: "A high school diploma from an accredited distance education school is comparable to a resident high school. However, you should always check with the college or university you wish to attend first. Often, if you say that you've received your diploma through a nationally recognized accrediting agency, it is likely that it will be accepted."

How do I ensure that my studies will be accepted by a college or university?

DETC answer: "The registrar or dean at a college or university has the final word, but DETC accreditation and recent evaluation procedures make a favorable decision likely. The American Council on Education reviews courses from many DETC member schools and makes credit recommendations, which are published annually in *The National Guide to Educational Credit for Training Programs.*"

When evaluating a program in the light of your own goals, another point to keep in mind is its practical results. Once the coursework ends, it's unclear how widely employers will accept dot-com diplomas. Recruiters are suspicious and wonder things like, "What's the difference between a cyberlecture and the Discovery Channel?" Acceptance may vary depending on the field. Law firms and academia may never fully embrace distance credentials; less conservative businesses may be more flexible. The military, public schools, and technical firms seem more accepting, especially of engineering or computer degrees. For the time being, though, if the diploma is critical to your career and life planning, you may want to stick with the distance offerings of well-established institutions, since degrees from established schools with bricks-and-mortar campuses appear no different from the traditional variety.

It's not that the venerable ivy-walled institutions are saintly and wholly service oriented. They may be nonprofits, but they need cash like everyone else. However, they have a history and an accreditation and evaluation system.

Behind the hype

Cyberspace is so hot that there's an often overenthusiastic effort to fill it—or to get a piece of it—fast. We're used to commercial ventures doing hard sells, perhaps even hooking us with not-quite-total truth; and as more commercial ventures enter the education field via high-tech networks, it becomes especially important to check their bona fides. Equally overenthusiastic, however, are those who want to sign on for a hot course no matter what. This is the time to get smart—to pay attention to your own common sense.

Follow the old-fashioned rule: if it sounds too good to be true, it probably is.

- *If they promise accreditation, check it.*

- *If they want your credit card number and personal information before they're willing to give you any information— click off.*

- *If the free information packet is full of wild promises, trash it.*

In Other Words

Remember to follow the dots: a program offered by a "name.edu" or a "name.org" is rarely likely to be a purely commercial venture and potential rip-off.

Why it matters

As easy as it is to find, sign on for, and pay for distance learning these days, it becomes even more important to choose the best programs for your needs. If you're choosing and paying for your own education, you want quality for quality's sake—not a waste of money or time. If you're signing onto a training program to meet your employer's needs—even if the employer is paying for it—if you get an inadequate course, the credits won't count. And increasingly, it's parents who are helping their kids find schools that include at least a distance component.

Voice of Experience

Parents of high-schoolers comment, "Helping our kids pick the right college is something that most parents assume to be of great importance. We want to be sure that the school is qualified to provide the optimum education for the money we're laying out. Anyone can put a course up on the Internet and have you click in your credit card number. One criterion of quality is licensing by the state or accreditation by independent boards."

Bottom line

Ask in detail about financial support for your educational adventure. Be sure you have the details of the costs—including the extra costs that may be incurred by any software (or even hardware) requirements. Be sure you get the straight word on what financial aid is available from the institution for part-time or nontraditional study, if that's what you're going for. Then ask around.

Are you ready? Spend some time now searching the Web. Find at least four (or more) education providers that match these requirements:

1. Gives you the kind of learning opportunity you want and need

2. Offers good student support

3. Is affordable

4. Is manageable, given the rest of your schedule

First, get the facts: questions about costs and payments are at least as important as those related to technology and content. Ask questions of other potential aid providers as well. There are plenty besides the federal government. Check some of the aid sites listed in Appendix D. See about scholarships from the school itself (most of these are for degree-seeking students, but you can never be sure—so check!). Go to associations involved with the subject areas you're studying—engineering, advertising, nursing, whatever. They have funds available. Ask the school. Ask your employer. Many employers reimburse employees for continuing education, whatever its format (and they may be very glad to have you learning without leaving the job). Unions, too, fund some education. Double-check with federal or state programs about Pell grants, special funding for minority groups or others with special characteristics, the G.I. Bill, and the Defense Activity for Non-Traditional Education Support (DANTES) program. You may also want to contact your state's higher education agency for information about additional aid.

Even before you explore the money angle, fill out the Free Application for Federal Student Aid (FAFSA), which you can do online. Any funder, private or public, will want to see that document, so be prepared. Finally, don't forget to ask about payment plans. Most legitimate providers will arrange for monthly payment plans, and with the new world of student-driven education, you are more likely to be able to take one or two courses at a time, so you can sign on only for the learning you can afford.

And now you may be ready to sign on, click in, and start learning. But you're more likely to click yourself into a successful experience if you can place it into a wider context. The next section can help you gain an understanding of the bigger picture.

Part 5

The Bigger Picture

So far the focus of the book has been on step-by-step practical matters—"all about you." This section of the book provides that kind of information, too—but the camera has panned back a bit to give a wider picture. Aspects of this scene affect your actions, too: awareness of issues surrounding teachers, training matters, and trends for the future will affect the decisions you need to make as a distance learning student. These chapters are designed to help you gain that awareness—and once you have those issues tucked into your belt, you're ready to use the checklist to do some serious planning.

Chapter 9

Teacher's Spot

Studying online, as earlier chapters have indicated, is often more challenging than the previously uninitiated imagine. So is teaching online: it's more than a matter of standing in front of a video camera and spouting a lecture. While it can be difficult cueing into a class one can't see, most teachers who put in the online effort report that opportunities outweigh obstacles. The advantages they note include being required to focus more intensely on preparation. They may also appreciate the fact that they can reach a wider audience, including students who would otherwise be unable to attend, and link them up with other students—and speakers—from a wide range of backgrounds. But even under the most ideal and idealistic circumstances, a number of issues can cloud the distance education picture. Understanding these can be of value in choosing, rating, and doing well in online study. This chapter details some of the issues, focusing on:

- *What special qualities distance teachers need—or need to develop*

- *What technical skills they need—or need to acquire*

- *What conflicts and questions arise from the new educational formats*

Voice of Experience

"I've spent a sabbatical semester and most of summer break working to create a really quality online course," comments a university professor. "I'm using Blackboard and it's very interesting and rewarding—but it's *very* hard work getting it right."

Why do such issues matter to you as a student? First, they can affect the quality of your education. On campus, you may have access to professor evaluation lists from fellow students; at a distance, you have to judge quality for yourself. Also, different viewpoints on distance education foster different teaching styles. Some teachers enjoy the process of addressing "classes by the masses" of hundreds or thousands at a time, while others stress the connected approach and work to personalize the distance experience.

In Other Words

"Connected Learning":

Technology can be used to create new learning environments and "opportunities." In this vision of "distance" education, learners and teachers connect better to information, ideas and each other via effective combinations of pedagogy and technology—both old and new. Learners, teachers, and related support professionals each have more opportunities to identify and improve effective combinations of: capabilities, needs, and goals of teachers; academic content; approaches to teaching and learning (pedagogy); and media and applications of technology.

Steve W. Gilbert, president of the TLT Group

Also, understanding the challenges distance instructors face may give you insights into dealing with them, since you can't do that apple-polishing in person. An instructor's skill in technology management may enable you to seek out education sources that have made use of professional help in presenting their material. At a distance, even more than in a classroom, a teacher may have something great to pass along, but may lack an appropriate style for reaching students successfully. Good teachers are increasingly learning good techniques via the special services now available (see Appendix A).

Finally, grasping conflicts over issues of ownership may also give you insights into how providers operate, and can offer clues to your own accreditation. Is a Harvard professor teaching that Harvard course? Is the individual presenting the material the one who developed it? And so forth.

What makes a good distance teacher

Summaries of commentaries about what characterizes good distance teachers include "teachers who are outstanding in *any* classroom" and have "learner-centered attitudes," and who are enthusiastic; are flexible and adaptable; and have an ability to learn new skills and student-centered attitudes, to act as mentors, and to maintain a sense of humor.

Fast Facts

American Society of Training Directors (ASTD) research has shown that instructors are reluctant to teach online for reasons that include the following:

Belief that distance learning isn't as good as the classroom experience

Fear of using the technology and appearing less than proficient

Lack of control because of the need to work as part of a team

Increasingly though, online work is a necessity, so efforts need to be made to help teachers get up to speed.

More specifically, it takes a lot of effort. Most teachers who try distance education either drop it fast or work hard to get good at it, because, at least at first, it takes even more time than traditional preparation. Teachers work hard to plan, develop, and present any course, but those who enter the cyberteaching world say it brings a new set of demands. Students (as well as potential teachers) might take note: here's what experts and experienced online teachers—as well as your fellow students—suggest as criteria for good online teachers.

- *They design their courses for distance learning. Even if the content is the same as that of a previous in-class course, they don't assume that training with traditional methods prepares them for teaching at a distance.*

- *They plan activities carefully and let students know the agenda in advance.*

- *They are comfortable with the technology and see it as a tool—a means to an end rather than an end in itself. They have practiced with the technology—whether e-mail, microphones, or Javascript—so they can make optimum use of it and help students as well.*

- *They guide students through the technological system and arrange for newbies (newcomers to the Internet) to go through an introductory course in how to use the technology—and the communication techniques made possible and necessary by that technology. For example, they start courses with clear discussions of communication rules, guidelines, and standards.*

- *They build in extra time for communication and for materials delivery. This is especially important. They also have backup and alternatives for technology glitches.*

- *They create a student support structure that allows students to communicate with the teacher and each other and to get all-important feedback and support on questions and assignments.*

- *They create systems and opportunities for group activities, discussions, and teamwork.*

- *They take extra efforts to involve all class members—and get to know them well enough to understand any cultural or language differences that each may be dealing with.*

- *They are prepared to take extra time, during extra hours, to have conferences with the class and to e-mail individual students.*

There are some don'ts that both students and teachers list. For instance:

Don't treat distance courses like traditional face-to-face courses. Instead, consider both the good and bad points of technological delivery.

Don't jump straight into course content. Instead, allow extra time to get to know the students and for students to learn the system.

Don't rely on straight lectures and talking heads alone. Instead, develop extra time for discussion and special interactive assignments.

Don't go it alone. Instead, be sure to have a good support structure available.

Voice of Experience

"The success of any distance education effort rests squarely on the shoulders of the faculty. In a traditional classroom setting, the instructor's responsibility includes assembling course content and developing an understanding of student needs."

Barry Willis, University of Idaho

Perhaps the most critical aspect of successful online education is good planning. This is true for any educational process, of course, but in the distance learning situation, plans must take in a wider variety of elements and establish a system of teamwork as well as systems for presenting individual curricula. Teachers and administrators can employ traditional principles of instructional design to create instruction specifically intended for distance education programs or to modify or adapt traditional courses for a distance format. The major difference should be the involvement of a team to present or distribute the instruction.

Other differences call for planning the media—but professionals recommend that learning goals and content be decided before technical media are selected (though when using specialized services, as described in Appendix A, this may be predetermined). Special considerations also require creating strategies for reducing the psychological distance and increasing the level of interaction between teacher and students and between groups of students when there are multiple sites. Experienced distance teachers note that interaction and closeness will not just happen, but must be specifically planned for, with special attention to the development of materials.

Just as in traditional classes, setting instructional objectives is important: teachers need to write them down and convey them to students so that the class will know where it is going. Having a clear idea of what's expected is particularly important in order to help distance students feel that they are not operating in a vacuum.

Good distance education relies on the following structure (does your provider provide support?):

- Facilitators create a bridge between the students and the instructor.

- Support staff aids in student registration, distributing materials and textbooks, scheduling, distributing grade reports, managing technical resources, etc.

- Administrators work closely with technical and support service personnel, ensuring that technological systems function properly.

Some other critical details for effective distance learning programs follow.

Curriculum considerations

Lesson plans should include hands-on training with the delivery technology for both teacher and students. A preclass session in which the class meets informally using the delivery technology and learns about technical support staff is useful. Teachers should also find ways to require students to use e-mail, postings, interactive chat—whatever the technology of the course—at an early stage.

For Web-based instruction, which allows learners to gain knowledge and skill more effectively than traditional methods, the simple transfer of lecture notes and the like is a waste. It is better to print this kind of material, which can be read in hard copy more easily. Instructors should:

- *Encourage communication through conferencing activities, with or without teacher participation.*

- *Add to the curriculum enhancements such as role-playing and simulations of events like historical debates to engage students and enhance learning.*

- *Provide source documents—or links to them—on the site. This adds depth to study and facilitates conference work.*

- *Suggest links and sources to allow students to explore at will with flexibility, then bring information and material back to the class discussion.*

Teaching tips

Remembering that, for the most part, effective distance teaching means the enhancement of existing skills in responding to the students, rather than the development of new skills, successful distance teachers employ the following strategies for meeting students' needs:

- Awareness that student participants have different learning styles in terms of physical skills as well as pacing and comfort in group settings, as compared with independent work

- Humanization of the course by focusing on the students, not the delivery system—and by introducing (and listing links for) case studies and discussion topics with local relevance and interest

- Use of concise presentations and direct questions that call for student response

- A relaxed style that comes from practice with the equipment and experience with the process by which teacher and participants gain comfort in using the system

It's a teacher's responsibility to generate interactivity and feedback. In a four-walled classroom, good teachers do that, but others can get by with simply lecturing. Not so at a distance: teachers need to find ways to be sure that their class members are "there" and engaged. To improve interaction and feedback, experienced teachers suggest the following:

- *Prepare preclass study questions and advance organizers to encourage critical thinking and participation by students.*

- *After initial requirements for electronic communication, have students maintain electronic journals to keep up skills and comfort with this form of communication.*

- *Keep in touch! In addition to electronic interactions, consider telephone office hours using a toll-free number. (Set evening office hours if most students work during the day.)*

- *Combine a variety of delivery systems for interaction and feedback: one-on-one and conference calls, fax, e-mail, video, and computer conferencing. Consider personal meetings, too.*

- *Contact each site (or student) every week if possible, especially early in the course.*

- *Take roll carefully to be sure students are actually there.*

Special situations

Technology also plays a role in teaching situations that don't rely exclusively on computers or the Web. For example, even in in-class education, high-tech aspects can serve as support mechanisms. On-site teachers can use tech support to set up a class e-mail alias, listserv, and/or class Web site. Instructors often find that students ask them questions via e-mail more often than in person, and e-mail messages may be answered at the instructor's convenience.

A class listserv can be used to send announcements, distribute answers to frequently asked questions (FAQs), and encourage online discussion of class material. Conferencing software, too, can facilitate student-to-student discussion, and a class Web site can contain such items as the syllabus and assignment schedule, lecture notes, assignments, old tests, supplementary readings, and links to other relevant Web sites.

When video technology—either interactive television or VCR tapes—is used, some special considerations include the following:

- *Make good use of TV's visual component, showing illustrations, charts, and the like, as well as active demonstrations of topics, including conducting experiments as needed.*

- *Use special techniques, including timing classes to fit (speaking takes longer than writing!); practicing in front of a live camera prior to class (tape the presentation and study it); and understanding the technology even if a technician is actually working the equipment. Prepare viewers for new terminology to be used in the program, and answer any questions regarding the technical equipment being used. (Informing students if there will be camera operators or technicians in the classroom will reduce any discomfort.)*

- *Plan as much variety as possible to avoid boredom with the "talking head." For instance, consider team teaching to allow for a change of voice, image, and presentation style— and use as many guest speakers as possible.*

- *When speaking, vary facial expressions, tone of voice, body movements, and eye contact with the camera to enhance communication. Humor, questions, and dialog also help. Present content in 5- to 10-minute blocks interspersed with discussion. Require various kinds of student involvement— watching, reading, writing, and talking—and vary the focus from the on-camera presenter to a receiving site group or individual.*

- *Designate students at distant sites to lead discussions or survey the room for questions. Assign discussion questions in advance and have the questions appear in writing on the screen. Encourage student-to-student interaction by asking an in-class student or a student from a distant site to respond to questions.*

Some distance learning is achieved via audio equipment. This requires special techniques as well, to take advantage of the medium's two-way interactivity and to reduce the disadvantages of the absence of a visual component. Audio teachers may find the following tips useful:

- *Use pre-recorded audiotapes instead of audioconferencing when simple information needs to be presented without interaction.*

- *Content should be presented in blocks of only 10 or 15 minutes, followed by opportunities for interaction and feedback.*

- *Organize the presentation carefully so that students can follow it. Using preview, presentation, and review techniques provides structure to instruction.*

- *Enhance audio content with visual material like illustrations, slides, or videotapes. This information can be distributed ahead of time by mail or electronic means.*

- *It's especially important to use materials like textbooks, course manuals, content outlines, and handouts to provide organizational framework and save note-taking time.*

For audioconferencing, in which students can interact via various forms of audio equipment, teachers note that it's important to find alternative means for establishing a classroom rapport. Similar to the situation with computer learning, suggestions include sending a welcome letter, course syllabus, relevant course materials, available resources, list of contact people, and the like to students—as well as a photo and a short biographical sketch of the instructor. (Have students exchange photos and biographical sketches, too.) Another good idea is conducting a precourse audioconference to discuss the technology and procedures for effective audioconferencing, then having students use audio techniques to introduce themselves to one another.

What teachers need

Ohio State University researchers into online and other forms of distance learning focused on the resources and planning required for optimum use of these new formats. They found that the types of resources required to meet the expressed need of the faculty or staff members fall into three categories:

"Someone to help me": different types of human assistance and ways to request support

"A place to do my work": physical and ergonomic settings that are technologically enhanced

"Virtual resources to help me": online tools and strategies for solving problems at one's own desk

The researchers found that educational institutions must create an "enabling environment" that permits experimentation within disciplines but also provides resources to support the entire technological enterprise. Faculty and staff need all the support possible to become both willing and able to develop new skills and knowledge for applying new technologies to the teaching and learning process.

When it all works, everyone is happy. Teachers who are successful at their online work find a lot of satisfaction in it. As one instructor at the virtual Jones International University (who also has a "day job") describes his work: "I don't have a dud in any of my classes." The classes work, the instructor says, because online students are more motivated than "folks who doze through classroom lectures." Nevermind that the instructor may have to respond to scores of e-mails after teaching several classes a day and before posting the next day's classes and assignments: it's worth the effort.

New knowledge

In sum, today's teachers at every level, from kindergarten through graduate school, must have new knowledge in wide areas—not just their own subjects and the new technology, but in such matters as new learning styles, as well. Some examples are:

- *New theories of pedagogy and how technology reinforces learning in the young and the old*

- *New techniques of cooperative and collaborative learning and teaching*

- *New concepts such as building an online learning community, with features constructed to support collaboration and transformational learning*

- *New styles and techniques for student assessment and course evaluation*

- *New styles regarding classwork and interaction*

- *New rules regarding research and the sharing of knowledge*

- *New student profiles—from the young, who have been computer-savvy since toddlerhood, to the old, who are entering, reentering, or continuing their learning experiences and who bring with them long backgrounds of knowledge and experience*

- *New goals for education in the lifelong continuum of learning*

So much for the good old Golden Rule days, where the tune of the hickory stick was all the teacher had to know! And all of this is in addition to the new technology a busy instructor must absorb. There are books, training sessions, and special training programs on campuses and in school systems as well as online to bring teachers up to speed. But how much expertise do teachers really need?

Technical assistance

What if a good teacher wants or needs to enter the new-style classroom and, for any of a variety of reasons, lacks what it takes to grasp or make use of the technology required? Today every college and postsecondary school needs to promise e-learning services; and the government's efforts to close the technology gap mean that most schools at every level are wired for electronic education. There are countless classrooms that need the human touch to bring their technology to life, but it's no longer acceptable to put a camera at back of a lecture hall or use other slapdash online projects and courses just to fulfill marketing, institutional, or even statutory requirements. Nor do schools or teachers need to rely solely on their own technological expertise or jury-rigged self-training to learn and create systems. New services exist to take care of all the technical details. They don't provide the instruction per se, but, rather, the structure within which the learning can be developed—and the capability for such technical enhancements as e-mail, document sharing, online tests, and real-time chat rooms.

Fast Facts

Education is one of the nation's largest industries. It always has been, even when only the "standard" teachers, classrooms, and supplies were counted. Today, it makes up 10 percent of the gross national product (GNP), with hundreds of thousands of new-style teachers plus equal numbers of technical assistants and billions of dollars invested in equipment and development. Looking ahead, the government predicts that the marketplace for online learning alone will reach $46 billion by the year 2005.

These new operations run the gamut of topics and markets. A few examples:

- *University Access, staffed with former television executives who help professors present courses for the Internet*

- *Pensare, an e-learning firm that helps other business professors repackage teaching to sell to the corporate training market*

- *Blackboard, developed in collaboration with faculty members of Cornell University and now one of the leading services for getting learning online*

- *Anslie Group Inc., the education and training industry's first Web-based full learning environment*

- *net.TUTOR, a personal guide created by Ohio State University to understanding the Internet, tools, search skills, research techniques, and other various topics (online self-assessment is also available).*

- *Web Teacher, a self-paced Internet tutorial that puts both basic and in-depth information about the World Wide Web at a teacher's fingertips*

And there's Eduprise, WebCT Training Resources, ed2go.com, click2learn.com, and a whole series of other service providers in education management.

Each of the many new course management services (CMSs) takes a slightly different approach to helping teachers create telecourses of all sorts. In general, CMSs provide services that cover courseware, library, delivery, registration, and tracking systems designed to allow any institution or teacher to create an online, interactive system of education using the Internet or an existing intranet within a virtual learning environment. For example, a classroom teacher with little technical expertise can download a CMS that includes streaming digital video clips; RealAudio clips; animations; a pop-up glossary; announcements and bulletin boards; course information and schedules; document creation without using Hypertext Markup Language (HTML); Net meeting software; forums for discussions and assignments; and a resource library.

You'll find details of these and other resources in Appendixes A and D. Visiting some of the CMS sites (listed on pages 223–230) may offer insights into how your techno-teacher provides the education you seek. Services like these not only provide technical known-how, but many also serve as "coaches" to help teachers organize online courses that bring subjects to life and avoid dry, bland presentations that turn students off rather than stimulating them.

New issues for teachers to deal with

Does all this mean that every teacher has to march into cyberspace? No. Just as there will always be a place in education for the traditional small, liberal arts campuses, so there will always be a place for teachers of the old school, playing traditional roles at which they excel. Not every individual is suited to the high-tech world. And that may be one of the personal new issues that teachers today have to deal with.

Teachers who do choose to step into the new-style classrooms find that the challenges they encounter are not only new but unexpected. Discussions of ownership and copyright issues crop up regularly both on the news and in Congress. These issues have direct effects on teachers and institutions and raise questions like the following:

- Do online universities diminish the stature of professors? *Many professionals fear so: seeing that the new-style schools divide professors' jobs into two functions—content experts, who write the curriculum, and instructional faculty, who actually present it—the American Association of University Professors is trying to protect professors' reputations and careers by various means, including working to prevent online colleges from winning accreditation.*

- Who's in charge of teaching? *In more traditional (if electronic) settings, the questions are about who owns a course. Some faculty members are signing on with high-paying electronic education distributors to spread their wisdom beyond their home campuses, while administrators at those campuses are suing to keep the material within the ivied walls. Who owns the knowledge? Can the college that pays the instructor's salary hold a copyright on it? Or is it the intellectual property of the teacher-creator? And is intellectual property the real issue, or is the real problem fear on both sides of losing control and status? Arguments about this will likely continue for a long time.*

- Is distance education only about money? *While the potential for widespread distribution of free learning to all who want it is touted by Internet boosters, in reality distance education (that which provides accreditation of any kind, anyway) costs and can cost big. In the long run, technology may reduce costs: it should, but there's a lot more to pricing than the actual cost of production. Distance education is the bright hope of social reformers, because great numbers of people need education in order to participate in the new world economy. So far, the interest in making money off the new forms of telecommunication outweighs the interest in making generous use of them. In any event, when the technology is being introduced and the systems developed, costs are high.*

- Is knowledge free? *There's a lot of talk about the new sharing of learning and knowledge, and some idealists contend that information out there is out there for everyone. Others call that plagiarism. Existing copyright laws apply to the Internet, but there's controversy about that, too. The Digital Millennium Copyright Act, enacted in 1998, required the copyright office to research the current copyright situation and "submit to Congress recommendations on how to pro-*

By the Numbers

A year's worth of graduate study at a "name" institution costs from about $9,500 to $20,000. Here's a list of fees for a semester of graduate study at a distance from a "name" university:

Off-campus tuition	$951 per credit hour
Video auditor tuition	$530 per credit hour
Transcript fee	$45 nonrefundable one-time fee
Video special application fee	$55 nonrefundable one-time fee
Graduate admission application fee	$55 nonrefundable one-time fee
Certificate program conferral fee	$100 nonrefundable one-time fee
Video course withdrawal fee	$96, plus prorated tuition and all nonrefundable fees
Course notes (if required)	$40 nonrefundable fee
Instructional computer accounts (if required)	$45 nonrefundable fee

Off-campus fees (choose your delivery method):

Personal set of course tapes for U.S. students	$350 nonrefundable per-course fee
Personal set of course tapes for international students	$700 nonrefundable per-course fee
PicTel videoconferencing fee	$175
Online fee (if available for course of your choice)	$175 for U.S. students; $350 for international students

In other words, costs can be higher off campus.

mote distance education through digital technologies, including interactive digital networks, while maintaining an appropriate balance between the rights of copyright owners and the interests of users." Recommendations were released in May of 1999, and debate continued on how best to revise the existing fair use provision of the copyright laws, which allowed educational institutions to reproduce copyrighted materials for the purpose of education. As distance learning expanded, it came into direct conflict with a 1976 revision to a law that limited the extent to which fair use can be applied to students in remote locations. Moreover, the application of the rule to material distributed by digital information systems (like the Internet) is the subject of heated debate among those who (1) create material, (2) want to distribute it commercially, and (3) are working to stimulate the growth of distance education—as well as all those in Congress whose job it is to make the changes in the Digital Millennium Copyright Act concerning ownership of distance learning content and control of the virtual classroom.

What do all these issues mean for you? If content developers are reluctant to create material for the Web because their work might not be protected, then they are less likely to develop programs for widespread distribution. On the other hand, if institutions and other distributors are strictly limited in their use of material, they are also less likely to take the content and format of lifelong learning to the extent that the technology would allow.

These are issues that affect teachers and teaching directly—and by extension affect you and the millions of other students and would-be students of distance education.

It's about you

As you work your way through your own online course, you may now have a better idea of how much work has gone into making it function. And the teaching factors discussed—expertise, technology, and ownership—don't just affect academic distance learning, but the brave new world of training as well. For some insights into that aspect of ongoing education, see the next chapter.

Chapter 10

Re: Training

Is there a difference between training and education? Educators would say yes; trainers might say no. Training is more related to instruction in specific skills, while education is thought of as broader and deeper. Both have a common goal, though: instilling learning in participants. From the student's point of view, we all need training—and will continue to need it. People are more likely to be "trained" than "educated," in fact. So the review here of the characteristics of effective training, the range of training, and the key to good programs should be of interest to most potential trainees—and trainers as well. This chapter also takes a look at the future of training—an area of education that has always been at the cutting edge of technological delivery.

Skills training, as compared with education, is the traditional goal of distance education (beginning with a shorthand course offered back in the eighteenth century); and while higher-level forms of education were plodding along in classrooms with rows of chairs, training sessions almost always had some technological component—whether it was the U.S. mail or early-morning TV shows. From filmstrips and overheads to satellite conferencing, today this is even more true: virtually all of the hundreds of thousands of training programs and providers in the country are heavily technological, with the majority conducted at a distance, and most of those via computer.

Fast Facts

Training magazine reports that the total budget for training in the United States was $62.5 billion in 1999, with $15 billion of that going to outside providers of training products and services. While not quite one-third of that went for information technology training, a growing percentage was for nontechnical topics. The market for Internet-based education is expected to reach $11.4 billion by 2003, up from $550 million in 1998.

While educators carefully differentiate themselves from trainers, training can be seen as leading the way to sophisticated, stimulating classrooms at a distance. Training is pervasive: one resource site alone lists 450,000 training programs offered by 10,000 providers, and another can point you to 120,000 more. And that's far from all of the freestanding programs led by people who make their careers as trainers, not to mention all the training programs provided in house by businesses large and small. Add to that all the self-help videos, paid TV programming, and instructions for programming computers or even installing curtain rods that now come to us on disks or videotapes. To say that there's a boom in training is to radically understate the situation. And, as in so many other boom times, there's a lot of hype and fast talk surrounding the events.

Add to the training story the fact that even the best of the most professional trainers have to hustle fast to keep up with the technology they need to use, and you'll see why figuring out which programs are valuable or to the point—or which are even needed—is tough for students and instructors alike.

Those who think they needn't bother with understanding the training scene are missing the point. Training is pervasive in the population. There are well over 50 million of us seeking training in any given year—so even if you have no thought of going back to school, chances are almost 100 percent that you will experience some kind of training (even slipcovers come with a how-to video).

Voice of Experience

The U.S. Office of Technology Assessment considers technology a valuable component of teacher education and professional development: "Today's technologies offer a means for moving beyond the old models of professional development to more flexible use of training resources and time; from 'one-size-fits-all' workshops to 'just-in-time' training and support."

The range of training

Once focused primarily on business practices, training picked up a lot of steam when the computer age brought demands for entirely new skills. With experts estimating that technical skills need upgrading every four years, this type of training will only keep booming. But, beyond that, training has moved into other areas of management and now extends into every area of commercial and professional life. Some examples of the kinds of technical training available now are:

- *Hardin Construction created its own education and training Web site because over half of its employees work away from the corporate office but still need education and training.*

- *Online training provider Ninth House Network takes a broadband local area network (LAN) approach to training, combining interactive learning tools with a sitcom-style video. The course changes every month and is used by the navy, the Justice Department, the IRS, and the Federal Aviation Administration.*

- *notHarvard.com creates courses that manufacturers can give away to encourage product sales (while it wages court battles over its name).*

Large corporations and small business alike increasingly turn to Internet-based training; electronic learning is the dominant form, because it helps employees get training for their particular needs on demand and at their own pace.

By the Numbers

Ninety-two percent of large corporations said they used some kind of online learning in 1999, according to the Masie Center, a technology and learning think tank. Making Internet education companywide is believed to be essential in the next several years because it gives companies the ability to attract younger workers and reach global workforces that cannot be brought together for training courses, the tools to deliver marketing education to teach salespeople about products, and the flexibility that allows employees to learn on their brief periods of downtime between obligations. Savings are also a big motive: IBM reports yearly savings of $175 million in its education budget, or $490 per student day, gained by using online teaching.

In another trend, corporations are forming learning partnerships with educational institutions—both online-only universities like Capella and Jones International and more traditional institutions. Federal funding is now being made available for public-private training partnerships. To illustrate the range of what training means in contemporary society, let's look at some other trends in training as reported by the American Society of Training Directors (ASTD), a leading organization for training specialists (and a good resource for information and referrals on training programs).

Customer-focused e-learning (CFEL)

The business of providing training to customers—whether they're businesses along the value chain or Web-connected consumers—is poised to explode. This new business model can shift e-learning from a support role to a role as a marketing tool and even a profit center. Companies from a variety of sectors are targeting not only their own workers but also their customers with e-learning offerings.

Changing content

Training programs used to be focused completely on technology. Now, however, computer-based programs place a lot of emphasis and discussion on management training—on "softer" skills like how to lead a group of technology employees or how to take advantage of management opportunities.

What it takes to create a training program

What goes into making up a training program? Think it's easy, just slapping up some how-to on the screen? Here are the elements in a contemporary training program. Start with facilities, trainers or instructors, visual aids, and study material. Then add test structure, organizational systems, course creation, and administrative efforts. The e-learning systems hired by corporations as well as colleges include programs like personal portal pages, individual course activity portfolios, online registration, hyperlinked tables of contents, question groups, optional time-out settings, automatic feedback on missed questions, templates to create course content without having knowledge of Hypertext Markup Language (HTML), and statistics and reports on participants.

A typical set of topics for a training program offered by a business includes items like:

Applications for technology

Communication skills

Compensation and benefits

Consulting

Emotional intelligence

General human resources

Instructional systems design

International and related resources

Internet search tips

Intellectual capital

ISO/Total Quality Management

Knowledge management

Language training

Leadership

Learning technologies

Learning theory and assessment tools

Management development

Performance improvement

Safety training

School-to-work

Skill standards

While other technologies—from videos to audio-workbook packages—are still used for training, online and/or Web-based systems are the most common, primarily because they are both cost effective and easy to schedule asynchronously.

Keys to quality

With many hundreds of thousands of training programs available, covering almost every topic imaginable in every variety of format, how does one judge the quality of a program? Whether consumer or provider, here are recommended points to keep in mind. The most worthwhile programs provide:

Interactive formats

Tutorials

Exercises, worksheets, and case studies, with ongoing feedback

Test and other assessment materials

Management systems, from registrations to reports

Relevant content

Careful planning

The best training programs result from thorough design: effective training requires a lot more than cobbling together a how-to. It's carefully planned, according to professionals, who describe a systems approach that includes a step-by-step approach like this one:

1. Preproject evaluation that identifies needs and solutions

2. User analysis that focuses on profiling both participants and instructors

3. Job description to gain information on the tasks performed by the target population

4. Content examination to review existing procedures and programs

5. Instructional planning—the actual drafting of the teaching program, from objectives through techniques

6. Materials development—creating the instructional materials

7. Prereview of materials—having others check the work and conducting pilot sessions

8. Presentation—using the materials and the program in the real setting

9. Evaluation—reviewing whether the instruction succeeded (did it accomplish its goals?), making changes accordingly

Plan of action

The bottom-line basics of any plan are assessment, design, implementation, evaluation, redesign, and working to plan training programs, but there's no "freeze-dry" pattern. The most important factors to consider are the actual goals and needs of the training program—whether you're signing up for something presented by your employer's human resource department, considering the purchase of a high-price firm's offerings for your company, or just signing on for a Web-based training (WBT) program on your own. Format and technology are great, but do they get you where you want to go?

In Other Words

Workplace education is a hot area for instructional systems design (ISD). There are no specific, identifiable skills to develop with this specialized teaching procedure: instead, results sought are often articulated in terms of awareness, understanding, and sensitivity—elements that may be hard to define and measure, but that are critical to job success in the fast-changing patterns of structure and process.

Quality faculty

No matter how expert people may be in their own fields, they don't necessarily have the competency to train others in them. People who try to train and aren't good at it aren't asked to do it again—but there are better ways of choosing than by trial and error. In some cases, you can trust the quality of the provider, especially if it offers demos, and there's word of mouth too. But trainers can also be certified—so consumers can select certified trainers and trainers can seek certification. Although most fields do not require certification for trainers, it's a sign of quality—and some consumers of training do insist on certification. Some certification programs include:

CDLI: Certified Distance Learning Instructor

CDLA: Certified Distance Learning Administrator

CDLI-A: Certified Distance Learning Instructor-Asynchronous

In addition, the U.S. Department of Labor has designed two labor certification programs for telecommunicator/distance educators in both synchronous or asynchronous delivery modes. Consumers may look for—or insist on—these credentials, and people who are serious about being trainers or distance educators may find that pursuing certification programs is a way not only of learning skills, but of demonstrating their serious intent. These programs are fairly rigorous and require a considerable commitment of time and thought. They are designed to develop skills in distance education techniques such as audiographics, videographics, Web-based instruction, computer-driven teaching, and/or administration, and require not only class attendance and report writing but hands-on experience as well.

How training courses work

Each training course is different, and all the resources available to make each one outstanding means that they all should be outstanding, perhaps. But putting together good courses can actually be more complicated because of all the opportunities and ingredients. Typical courses combine state-of-the-art technology with other components that might include online admissions information, an online course catalog, and links to libraries and other research resources with content specifically designed for the business, government, or education unit seeking training. As is the case with colleges, there are now course management systems through which experts in any given field can provide content to fill the structures designed by the services.

There are also prepackaged programs for training at a distance that focus on specific topics. A few examples:

- *Oracle Learning Architecture offers courses in Oracle database, UNIX, Windows NT, and much more for a registration fee.*

- *eTraining helps professionals prepare for and pass Microsoft certification exams. Subscriptions include audio-narrated presentations, sample exams, and online discussion forums.*

- *ReCor Corporation offers a course in NBT for Lotus Notes.*

- *ByteK Designs Inc. provides cybereducation for systems and IC design.*

- *Digital University, Inc. offers over 40 courses as well as links to additional courses and to regulatory, legal, and operational information sites. Courses are exclusively designed for financial institutions including commercial banks, savings institutions, mortgage banks, and credit unions.*

- *Edge Interactive delivers comprehensive training on technical systems; installation and maintenance; business applications such as Oracle and SAP; hardware and software products; and end user skills.*

- *Genentech Inc. provides online learning environments for high school biology students and teachers.*

- *IBT Financial, Inc. offers 18 Internet-based training courses for the financial services industry. Courses are accredited for continuing education hours by 16 state insurance boards and the Institute of Certified Bankers.*

- *Intuition Publishing is a computer-based training company that specializes in financial training. Its financial training and reference products are used by more than 150 banks and financial institutions in 52 countries.*

How to find a training program

Students looking for a training program—or potential trainers looking for a place to promote their programs—may feel confused by all the opportunities out there. Searching by topic through the Web is one approach, but going to an associated source is more effective. Among these are groups like TrainSeek.com, which calls itself an "independent e-commerce web site designed exclusively for corporate trainers and other managers." TrainSeek.com finds and reviews training products and lists them by type and rating on a single Web site.

THINQ (formerly TrainingNet) is another site with a fairly similar service. But the leader is the ASTD, which is a nonprofit association of trainers and training programs. The ASTD provides guidelines and links to professional training programs led by professionals who must qualify for membership in the association. It also furnishes expert information to members and nonmembers alike, which may be of value to both users and providers. For example, the ASTD's Web-based library services offer personalized research on training, human resources, and workplace performance topics including facts about training expenditures and consultant fees; links to other professionals; and reading lists on a wide variety of topics relevant for trainers and trainees alike.

Into the future

Training is so cutting-edge in the world of distance learning (indeed, it's always been the pioneer in these fields) that it's hard to imagine the future being much different from the high-tech present. But forecasters look ahead to new forms of training and find, for example, that as broadband Internet connections become a household fixture, every individual of every age and interest will have easy, direct access to expert training in almost any field.

A major change will be in content. Beyond the information technology field, businesses of all sorts are using technology to improve training, lower costs, and reach target audiences as companies broaden their horizons to customers as well as employees. Net training providers such as IBM and Caliber increasingly turn to colleges and universities for educational content to offer to employees and customers. For example, many of IBM's customers include the manufacturers, financial service companies, and petrochemical firms that make use of IBM products.

The uses to which training will be put will continue to change and make increasingly dramatic and widespread inroads into society as a whole. For example, customer-focused e-training provides training to customers—whether they're related businesses or Web-connected consumers. This type of training is becoming commonplace—and a sign of a truly with-it business (just as a Web site once was). In fact, you're probably in training now—and if you're not yet, you soon will be, if you're a customer of almost any sort: it's predicted that by 2003, more than 40 percent of e-learning activities will be aimed at external customers, rather than employees or clients.

Throughout our society, education and training—in particular e-learning (electronically at a distance)—is becoming the standard in many new ways. The reasons are simple: products and services—from cameras to software—are getting more complicated. Already, self-service Web sites offer hundreds of features, and software itself is so sophisticated that it requires its own training programs. We won't buy services and products that we're afraid we can't use—so the training comes not with the products but ahead of them. What's next?

By the Numbers

By 2003, at least one-tenth of all buyers of high-technology products will have learned how to use them before purchase, according to the Gartner Group.

Building learning into products: Microsoft is a pioneer of that—with its Office software providing no fewer than a half dozen CFEL training devices labeled "help tools." Answer Wizards and Alerts Brokerage were also early major providers of this kind of training—making it less scary to invest online for people who had never invested at all. Soon this kind of CFEL will make a difference in which company's products are bought and which are left on the shelf.

Not all this new customer training is canned or built in, either: one increasingly common variety of CFEL is the prerecorded, streamed-on-demand presentation, typically using a high-profile speaker and high production values. Much like a keynote address or high-profile press conference, these presentations can launch new offerings, position a company in the context of its competition, or simply provide information on how best to use a company's products or services. This form of CFEL is most often offered by e-commerce companies, and is already quite elaborate. E-businesses also now sponsor virtual seminars, with experts addressing participants/customers live via the Internet.

What do these brand-new formats for training mean for the training industry—and for us as customers of more traditional training? They make us more demanding as customers of all sorts. As we come to expect expert training with our products, we will resist buying from companies that provide no training.

As noted at the beginning of the chapter, we're all already clients for training—and whether we ever feel a need for schooling or not, we will be perpetual trainees. As training becomes part of our daily routine, we will become even more particular about the quality of the more formal training we select.

But the basics of selecting that training, whatever its format, remain simple. To sum up quality training from the point of view of student and instructor:

Is the content what's needed?
Is the instructor qualified to teach the subject?
Is the format accessible and appropriate?

Selecting a training program is important—and it's something you'll be doing a lot in the future.

Chapter 11
Looking Ahead

Online learning is not a fad. It's not even speculation to say that it will continue to expand and extend itself throughout our culture. Here's a quick review of the reasons:

Technology both drives the need for continuous education and allows for it—not just because it enables more people to access education, but because education is increasingly a requirement and bricks-and-mortar classrooms cannot in any way keep up with the demand.

Demographics and economics means we're living longer and working harder. Demographically, it's a sure bet: the younger generation is computer-connected already, and surveys indicate that seniors want to keep learning but don't want to go back to school.

In this chapter we will touch on the highlights of what to expect in the population, formats, and technology of learning for the future. Things are changing fast—so fast that the scene and its opportunities for connections have probably changed since you started reading this book. They have surely changed since the writing of the book. One thing will not change, however—you will be continuing your studies.

Demographics

People recognize the need to continue learning well past school age. Adults over age 50 are enthusiastic about learning, but don't want to go to class, according to a survey of more than 1000 older adults recently made by the American Association of Retired Persons. But you needn't wait for your golden years to plug into the future of education. Distance learning makes education available to many people who had been cut off from it before, since it allows isolated people to gain an education and permits those who have to work to afford it (the majority of college students today) to fit study into their workday. Not only do most of us have to work to pay for college education—but we working adults are the ones, surveys show, who account for the rapid increase in Web-based training (WBT), which is expected to grow exponentially, as noted in the previous chapter.

What do these factors mean for you? If you're at the stage of just considering your first online program, it means you're probably at the beginning of a lifelong project, so you can expect to continue. It also means that, even as the technology gets more sophisticated, it will be easier to access for non-techies. But this tidal wave of high-tech learning also means you need to be a better judge of content. As noted in Chapter 9, a major issue in the brave new world of learning is what—and whose—education is being conveyed. In the midst of all the surrounding buzz, learning itself might be lost, so the consumer needs to remain alert for quality content and usable formats.

Technology

Here is some of the technological wizardry you might expect to encounter as you embark on your twenty-first-century learning journey:

- *The U.S. Department of Education reported in 1999 that 60 percent of all 1997–1998 distance learning programs were offered over the Net, and that the fastest-growing education technology was Internet based. According to* The Futurist, *95 percent of instruction in the United States will be digitally enhanced by 2025.*

- *In May 2000, tech industry leader Intel announced plans to invest over $200 million in developing a streaming media business that will provide the infrastructure to enable media providers to stream concerts, films, briefings, and other content over the Internet. The Internet Research Group estimates that by 2004, the market for streaming media services will grow to more than 20 times its current size, reaching $2.5 billion.*

Formats

Snazzy as the new technologies may seem, the biggest actual change will be in future formats for education. For example, U.S. Department of Labor statistics, published in the book *Workforce 2000,* show that the workforce is becoming older, less advantaged, and less literate. Therefore, if business and industry are to compete, survive, and prosper in today's highly competitive global environment, continuous training and retraining is critical. One key to success is the application of cost-effective and continuous means of distributing that training. As a result, distance learning will be tightly woven into all aspects of our culture. Exactly how this will happen is where the debate starts. On the one hand, we have predictions like this one from Dr. William Draves of the Learning Resource Network:

> There will be 1,000 participants per class. The average fee will be below $100. Participants will come from all over the world. There will be more interaction online than in person.

while others like Steven Gilbert of the TLT Group focus on personalizing what they call *connected education.*

Will there be universal computer linkage? Perhaps. While many Third World countries complain that the West is overly focused on technological advances to the exclusion of more basic issues, India has placed intense efforts into the expansion of Internet use: in three years, Internet service expanded from 4 million to 23 million users, with rapid expansion in rural as well as urban areas to build business and enhance education.

What will the future university look like?

- *Stating that access to electronic resources is what matters in modern scholarship, management professors at Purdue University want to get rid of the book stacks in a library they share with agricultural economists—who insist that they still need access to their scholarly heritage as embodied in printed works.*

- *Drexel University has created a wireless campus, allowing students and faculty members to roam across the university's 22-acre physical campus while connected to the Internet. The Philadelphia university used transmitters fixed to walls inside buildings, as well as about 20 antennas, to cover the campus in a single network. Drexel was one of the first to establish a fully wireless campus, but other universities, including Carnegie Mellon and Wake Forest, are catching up quickly.*

- *Beginning with the class entering in fall 2000, St. Mary's University in San Antonio, Texas, provides incoming freshmen with notebook computers. The university believes that this "promotes learning experiences based upon the following types of interactions: faculty with students; students with other students; and students with resources such as books, journals, experts, and other dynamic electronic sources."*

In many ways, technology is changing the shape of higher education in more ways than delivery systems. The rules that governed education in the past—like those regarding financial aid, for instance (see Chapter 7)—don't really fit for the future and may actually interfere with a student's successful participation. Faculty and administration are dubious about high technology on campus, but when approached respectfully, they are willing to incorporate it. For example, a 1999 University of Illinois study presented a much improved faculty assessment of online learning as a result of campus efforts to stress the need for quality relationships between teachers and students, whether the interaction takes place face-to-face or on the Web. Similarly, The American Council on Education (ACE) recently published a document recommending that colleges and universities around the country revise key campus policies to accommodate online distance education.

Administrative glitches will clear up fast. Even now, nearly half of higher education institutions engage in online distance learning. As a group, these institutions spent more than $1.5 billion in 1998 (a 300 percent growth rate). Penetration of campus networks has reached 83 percent for higher education as a whole, and half of all college students own personal computers, making online education as much an on-campus phenomenon as a distance learning trend. Ohio State researchers recently concluded, ". . . there appears to be agreement across all colleges that greatly enhanced use of the Web, networked computers, and the infusion of technology in the classroom with the use of liquid crystal display (LCD) projectors and other presentation hardware is foreseen and nationally, more university courses are using more technology," from e-mail to the Net.

The same forces are bringing education into entirely new forums and formats:

- *In spring 2000, bookseller Barnes & Noble announced a partnership with notHarvard.com, a company that creates online courses, to offer a free online "university" for its customers—the latest in a series of efforts by businesses to attract and retain customers by offering them a form of free education. (Although companies like notHarvard.com have adopted the terms* courses *and* universities *to describe what they do, their offerings are more like how-to demonstrations at businesses than traditional college courses.)*

- *Rupert Murdoch linked his News International company with the 18-member university network Universitas 21 in a move to enter the rapidly growing global market for online higher education.*

- *Some for-profit education companies use the lure of Web-based education just to sell products, according to the Institute for Higher Education Policy. This trend will likely continue, but the Institute is studying ways to define quality measurements for Web-based learning in the future.*

- *Other new-style linkages now connect textbook publishers to universities and online institutions. For example: Caliber Learning Network has announced a partnership with the college division of book publisher John Wiley & Sons to develop Web-based business courses. Delivery platform provider WebCT will be teaming with college publisher Houghton Mifflin to develop college-targeted e-learning.*

- *America Online (AOL) launched a free online service aimed at schools in May 2000.*

- *On-campus electronic communication now creates student need for 24/7 technical support, according to the* Chronicle of Higher Education, *which notes that many students who enroll in online programs complete their coursework at hours when the traditional campus is closed and become easily frustrated waiting hours or even days for a simple problem to be resolved. In turn, this demand for full-time technical support is spreading through society as a whole.*

- *The private sector is eyeing higher education's $240 billion in revenues as a target for investment. Shares in the University of Phoenix are already traded on the stock exchange. Investors seek a profit from schools like these, but concern rises that for-profit education companies will hire faculty away from traditional universities in the future.*

- *The Corporate University Xchange notes that the funding model of corporate universities has changed; they've become profit centers, not just employee service arms. Higher education is a stagnant market, except for working adults—so there's stress on the value of continuing education. Innovative solutions presented by corporate and university partnerships make financial sense for both parties.*

- *"College" has been extended beyond the traditional four years, as higher numbers of employees and management executives attend postcollege training that focuses on corporate issues, or so-called corporate universities. The number of corporate universities has increased from 400 in 1988 to 1600 currently, according to the Corporate University Xchange.*

Voice of Experience

While in the navy, Glenn Jones tried to learn Russian by correspondence, but the experience was frustrating and led him to search for a better way to educate the masses. In the 1980s he started offering classes via cable TV. Then, in 1995, he founded Jones International University, a campusless college whose employees work in a Denver office park. Classes take place in cyberspace, where the regionally accredited school offers bachelor's and master's degrees. The school began with 125 degree-seeking students; founder Jones says, "There's no reason we couldn't have a million students."

The quality conundrum

Meanwhile, debate goes on about whether distance education is as good as the old-fashioned kind. Many recent studies have shown no significant difference between what students learn in a classroom or far away. But most of those studies deal with television courses; Internet courses are new enough that research is still evolving. Earlier studies have been questioned—more research is needed and will likely continue indefinitely. Again, though, successful distance learning depends on the student—and it's up to you to know if it's right for you.

Likewise, as online learning expands and administrators of school budgets search for ways to squeeze out more from less, easy access to additional learning is welcomed by the educational community. It remains up to the student to pick wisely, because providers are more often than not in a rush to get an educational product on the market. Colleges should be more patient in their drive to put courses online, says the president of the McGregor School at Antioch University in Seattle, Washington. Meanwhile, widely touted institutions like Western Governors University have experienced setbacks due to not being granted accreditation. Patience and caution might be a trend in themselves. Planning is definitely called for—but in the meantime, even the institutions slower to adopt high-tech higher education will inevitably be affected. For example, while many education dot-coms may not rank high on the scale of higher education quality, they have caused education consumers to demand more services from more traditional schools. Traditional higher education institutions will have to adapt, so even on the old-fashioned campuses, we're likely to see plenty of changes. And even those that are racing to put anything up on the screen are recognizing the need to plan thoroughly for new ventures. Key to creating good programs is preparing the groundwork with appropriate resources and a solid infrastructure.

Distance education as a whole is sending ripples through the way all higher education is organized. Administrators from leading distance education institutions told a congressional commission that federal regulations governing financial aid and accreditation discourage additional use of technology for teaching, and urged changes in the regulations governing distance educators.

Future formats

Canada's TeleCampus is offering more than 12,000 courses to students in 22 countries. The United States Open University, a not-for-profit university providing high-quality part-time education, is the sister institution of The Open University, established in 1969 in the United Kingdom by Royal Charter. The Open University is the United Kingdom's largest educational institution, with more than 164,000 students enrolled in 41 countries. The United States Open University has adopted The Open University's Supported Open Learning method, which is specifically designed for learning at home and at work. Unlike many distance learning programs in the United States, which are based on a single method of course delivery (e.g., Internet learning or television), those offered by The United States Open University will combine a variety of learning media (print, videos, CD-ROMS, online services, software, etc.). Six of the world's top educational institutions, including Columbia University and the London School of Economics and Political Science, have formed Fathom, a for-profit Internet site that will offer its own college courses. The site will also offer courses from other colleges and universities.

In the world of corporate/university partnerships, the Corporate University Xchange found that the amount of time a corporate university has existed determines the following partnership tendencies:

- *Two years or less: corporations most often partner with four-year colleges or other companies.*

- *Three to 10 years: corporations frequently form alliances with other companies or with distance learning vendors for training.*

- *Ten-plus years: corporations tend to partner with distance learning vendors or business schools offering executive degrees.*

- *The most solid companies become education providers in themselves.*

A sampling of partnerships shows that Fortune 500 companies and major universities are involved, as well as private companies. For example, Lucent Technologies' corporate university—The Center for Excellence in Distance Learning—is involved in collaborative training programs with the University of Wisconsin Extension, Penn State, and Indiana University. These alliances provide distance learning workshops. Other linkups include:

- *New York University's School of Continuing and Professional Studies offers online courses in an alliance with IBM. In addition, NYU offers noncredit, online courses to corporate training programs through its extension school, the for-profit NYU Online.*

- *Pensare, a for-profit education company, offers an online master of business administration (MBA) program in alliance with the Fuqua School of Business at Duke University.*

- *SmartForce is providing "Smart Courses" to 7 of the 11 universities comprising an academic consortium known as the Committee on Institutional Cooperation.*

Voice of Experience

A corporate middle manager has embarked on an alternate route to an MBA. He's currently pursuing an employer-sponsored MBA online with Capella University. "I can't show up to class, say on a Monday or a Tuesday, and stay there for three hours," he explains. "[The partnership between Honeywell and Capella] is the only way I can get the degree, and what's more, the courses bring in everyday examples from our jobs. On most nights, I have dinner with my family, I watch the news, and then I go to my home office and log on. Right now I'm taking a marketing course. I order the course books over the Internet, and I submit my assignments over the Net as well."

Not long ago, formats like those would have seemed beyond imagination. Now they're taken for granted. What makes them possible, of course, is the technology—and that's what's moving the fastest. What's next? Look for:

- Online demos of e-learning offerings. *Providers of e-learning are adding to the numbers and sophistication of their online product and course demonstrations. Many content developers offer sample courses on their Web sites; DigitalThink and NETg, for example, allow users to take a free course. Some public learning portals, such as click2learn.com, also offer a free course from one of their content partners. Synchronous e-learning providers all schedule demos of their virtual classroom products with would-be customers.*

- Conference Webcast services combining video streaming, multimedia content, and interactive capabilities. *Businesses and schools can now extend the reach of their meetings over the Internet with Conference Webcast, a new offering from WorldCom Conferencing that combines live and recorded video with multimedia content and interactive capabilities.*

- Increased bandwidth. *Through 2004, more than 50 percent of consumers will still access the Internet at slow dial-up speeds. Many remote workers now rely on standard modems with connection speeds of 56 Kbps or slower. Higher production values, including streaming video, have to be managed carefully and leveraged. However, broadband connections are increasingly available throughout the country, allowing access to multiple communications sources at one's home phone and keyboard.*

On the other hand, "Not all of God's children are sharing in technology," says Martin Luther King III, referring to the "digital divide"—the idea that technology is widening the chasm between the haves and have-nots. Closing the digital divide is a major national goal for government and big business, and schools and libraries are being connected across the country, with Congress spending $5 billion on efforts to get public schools and libraries the wiring they need to be computer ready. For every kid to have access to a computer, an estimated $20 billion more may be needed, though Cisco Systems, Microsoft, and other companies are working to provide such access. The future will come eventually.

Looking ahead, it's likely that wireless Internet access, miniaturization, and similar innovations already in the works will make it possible for you to study not only for the rest of your life, but from wherever you are. (Dick Tracy, move over: if his two-way wrist radio had been real, he might have been able to make a career change.) Tomorrow's—and today's—technology may be mind-blowing, but you still have to use your mind to pick quality in content—and to do the work that will make your learning experience successful. While technology itself may be racing ahead of even imaginations, yours may not. You'll still be able to use tapes and TV; and remember—before you log on or click to pay for that course with your credit card, be sure you have the technology required. The providers will tell you what's needed. If they don't, find another provider. Your future is now. The next section will detail what it takes to happily get that online A.

Checklist: planning considerations

Now that you've had a chance to fit the facts of distance education into the broader picture of lifelong learning, you may have gathered some new factors—from teaching credentials to training resources—to consider as you evaluate your online learning needs and plans. Recognizing that the courses you select right now are likely to be only part of a longer (even lifelong) process, here's a chart to help you with some long-term planning.

DID: do it differently?				
If you've taken a course, what would you do differently?				
What questions will you ask future providers?	Credentials:			
	Program linkages:			
WIN: what is next?				
End goal for your learning program:	Learning credential:			
	Timetable:			
Next program: Format?	Web	Video	Audio	Other
Link to goal?	Credit	Noncredit	Certificate	

Part 6

How to Succeed at a Distance

It should all be making sense by now. No matter how many gadzillions of courses are available, no matter how high the tech and how complicated the initials and acronyms, deciding on the best distance learning approach for you is just a matter of gathering information and making decisions one at a time.

Getting into and through the educational process itself is also a simple (if not easy) step-by-step process. In this section you'll get tips and firsthand advice on how to go step by step to get from application to A. Chapter 12 takes you through the distance education process, from exploration through exams. Chapter 13 helps you manage the classroom scene—classwork, classmates—and the teacher. Chapter 14 helps you get down to basics with yourself, and Chapter 15 helps you review what you've learned about how to find and proceed with distance learning—plus tips on how to study skillfully and succeed with your own study plan. (If there are words or phrases here you still don't understand, refer to the glossary at the back of the book.)

Chapter 12
Following Procedure

Each course is different, but the elements are similar. In the most effective distance course, you can manage everything at a distance, from inquiries and selection through application and registration to final exams. In some environments, you may have to do some "face time" for some of the steps. In any case, here's how to get into class and get through it successfully.

The most effective educational Web sites will take you through this process, beginning with an overview. If you don't find this kind of information, you may want to reconsider signing on with the provider. Keep in mind that distance learning is, at its best, very personalized. The most effective providers are the ones that, even at a distance, offer you the most personalized help. That said, here's what you can expect as you enter the process of learning online.

Processing your education step by step

Whether you're in line for a noncredit class, a refresher course, or a full credit program, you'll need to proceed through pretty much the same set of stages: the process is similar to the old-fashioned kind of enrollment—with the big difference, of course, that there are no long lines to drop/add or to pay the bursar.

Here are the steps that students have taken probably since formal education was invented. They may be zippier with your super-fast modem, but they're all still there:

Exploration
Application
Advisement

Course selection

Registration

Payment

Textbooks

Coursework

Term papers

Labs

Exams

Sound familiar? Good—that makes distance learning a lot less mysterious. Here's how each of those old familiar steps works in the distance context, whether the school is offering the program on its own or via a packager. (Note that a lot of these steps apply to specialized training courses as well. For some special tips, see Chapter 10.)

Exploration

No heavy catalogs to overload your mailbox; just find your possible schools and click. You can find your ideal distance program (educational or training) by searching according to geography, course topic, types of credits offered, format (all online, or two-year, or intensive training, for instance), or a combination of any or all of those. You might go the education sections of the major search engines like Yahoo! or Excite—or go to the specialized education searchers, like those listed in Appendix D. For instance, if you want an associate's degree in early childhood psychology that you can complete while holding your current job, you'll want a distance education program that you can take through a community college—probably one not far from home, because you'll likely have to put in some face time as part of the training. You can find your best possibilities in just a few minutes online. If you're not online yet, you can do all this from a library or from job centers that many states and areas operate.

Use the same process no matter what educational goals you're focused on. Once you've got some names, you can, in most cases, narrow your search by specifying costs and schedules. Then, find the most likely sites and take a virtual campus tour. During your visits, keep chapter 8 handy to remind you of what to look for and ask about. And keep aware of how student friendly the site is. Is it easy to move around? Are you given step-by-step help? Can you do a demo? (If you have problems with any of these things, you're better off clicking elsewhere.) Go through the checklists in chapter 7— you can learn a lot firsthand before you even sign on. For training programs, follow the same procedure, only start at the training organization sites like those listed on page 255 or go to your professional association's or union's sites and find topics that interest you; then follow the links to various providers and check out the training programs that are available.

One big difference in this kind of education shopping is that you'll not only need to know about the school and the offerings, but also the equipment you'll need. The most helpful sites will tell you in advance. And even those that don't detail the information will clue you in simply by the equipment it takes to browse the site. If your browser has problems with the demo, chances are you're going to need an upgrade to actually take the course. Does the provider tell you what and how?

As an example of the kind of useful information you'll need, this techno-detail is offered by Northern Arizona University (NAU):

> Internet web browsers run best on fast machines with lots of memory and disk space. It will be necessary to get an Internet Service Provider or use NAU-PPP software.
>
> PC users running Windows 3.1 or Windows for Workgroups should seriously consider upgrading to Windows 95 or better. Macintosh users running anything less than System 7.5 should also think about upgrading their system software.
>
> **Be sure to check out the information on the homepage of your course for any additional hardware or software requirements.

The site also includes checklists of minimum configuration necessary for Web-streamed and Webcast courses.

You may want to make some decisions ahead of time based either on what equipment you'll need to get or what programs run on the machines you already have. If you don't have proper equipment, what suggestions do the providers offer? Can you use library equipment? What about a grant or loan to buy your own?

When you've narrowed down the possibilities to the ones that best answer your questions (and have found out whether you can do all that at a distance or whether you will need to go on campus), you're ready to proceed to the next step.

Application

In some cases, as for a training course or a noncredit program, your "application" simply requires a click, and (if you are confident the site is secure) the entering of your credit card information, if that's what you choose to do (see notes on privacy on page 171 and in Part 7). However, if you're planning on a more elaborate educational venture, the process will be more complex.

Following are examples of how some different sites instruct their prospective students. The State University of New York (SUNY), which maintains the SUNY Learning Network (SLN), accessible via all of its colleges and community colleges, suggests that SLN applicants "work with their advisor on their home campus to make sure they fulfill the requirements of the degree program," and via its Web site answers questions such as:

Will my home campus accept the credits I earn from taking an SLN course?

If you are a matriculated student at one campus and are interested in registering for an SLN course offered by another institution, you will need to adhere to that campus' transfer credit approval policy. You should check with your advisor for specific issues on transfer credit and applicability of course work toward the degree programs.

The University of Pennsylvania makes things clear for its distance PennAdvance students considering application to its programs:

Current or past students may register for a PennAdvance course either online or on paper. A full application is not required for students in these categories, and there is no registration fee. You may register online or download and print out a registration form using Adobe Acrobat.

Applications

Prospective students who have not previously applied for or taken a PennAdvance course must apply to the program. This includes post-secondary/college undergraduate applicants as well as high school/precollege applicants. Click here to apply or to view more information on the application process. . . .

Online learning is supposed to be simple, so the application process should be clear. You must assume that, for credit college programs, you'll still have to submit test scores, transcripts, and a portfolio of materials—so it's likely you'll need a face-to-face interview. But the process should be detailed for you.

Advisement

A distance student is entitled to the same kind of counseling as an on-campus enrollee; in fact, experts suggest even more in-depth advisement than for standard students (though more often than not, this is one step where both student and school fall short). In some cases, this service can be performed at a distance, too: in addition to the usual kinds of advice, students can get guidance about whether they're suited to the distance format and whether the courses they're considering are completely via distance education or whether they'll have to arrange some campus visits, as for labs or tests. Surprising as it may seem (and you've probably discovered this by now during your exploration of sites), some online programs offer little of this academic service—or none at all: they seem to expect you to pick a course, plunk down your funds, and proceed. Not a good idea! Even noncredit training programs can seriously waste your time if you hook up with the wrong ones.

Fast Facts

Experts note that advising and counseling often require attention to issues that are unique to distance learners. The obligations that compel students to take distance courses might carry job- or family-related pressures such that students may require special counseling for help with managing time and coping with varied responsibilities. Because distance learners are often returning to school after years of absence, significant pauses in their education might need to be remedied.

Voice of Experience

What format fits you best? Online administrators explain different systems: some courses may allow easy entry and easy exit in terms of when the class begins and when it ends. Some are totally canned or taped; those that most consider more effective involve a real live instructor and interaction with fellow students to create a valid educational experience. Teachers of distance courses can actually be available more frequently than on-campus professors. Other programs run online courses over a full academic term (whenever it starts). This allows students time to cover and assimilate the material, collaborate with fellow students learning the same topics at the same time, and work on projects and papers at a reasonable rate. Spreading a course out over 10 to 15 weeks also suits the many adult learners who are carrying many other responsibilities and have only a limited amount of time to devote to their studies.

A lack of advisement is a reason not to sign on at a site. It's also probably a big explanation for why the dropout rate is higher at a distance: people start a course and have to discover for themselves that it's not for them.

Here's a student's description of some worthwhile course counseling:

> NJIT provided a departmental advisor who helped me formulate a program of study, which mapped what DL [distance learning] courses would satisfy the course requirements for the degree program. Once this list was developed, the DL department would forecast what

courses were going to be given in upcoming semesters, and I then planned out the next two or three semesters. I feel that it's the individuals who administer the program that make a true impact on the success of the experience. NJIT's DL program has evolved into a great program.

In just about each course there was an orientation session, where the students and instructor could meet and discuss the goals of the course and pertinent information. In many cases the students are not in proximity to the college (thus the reason for taking the courses in the DL format in the first place).

If you're studying for credit, it's also critically important to determine your status vis-à-vis other schools or programs: will your credits for this course be recognized?

Advisement should also be clear about such "picky" but important details as financial aid, transcripts, and requirements. Check with your advisor for specifics on the various issues prior to enrolling.

If you have two or more online classes to choose from in order to meet your requirements, you might want to select the ones that offer:

Goals and objectives in advance

Lessons delivered in an interactive format

Tutorials

Exercises and case studies

Assessment materials to measure results

Course selection

Just as on an old-fashioned campus, you'll lay out a study plan that meets the requirements of your program—which are a prerequisite for what? Sign on for the courses that interest you the most. One advantage you have over students in the old-fashioned system is that you can easily avoid scheduling conflicts. And, while it may be harder to get word-of-mouth skinny on the prof, you may actually be able to sit in on a class.

On your high-tech campus, there's another step in course selection: being sure your equipment and system are compatible and up to the job of processing your coursework. Most experienced distance schools will take you through a process of checking out your system needs with a "test your system" segment on the school's Web site.

Registration

You'll also, of course, get instructions about details on how to register for courses or a training program. You'll want to know, for example, if you have to sign on at one particular time or place. On most asynchronous networks, students can sign onto their courses at any time of the day or night from any place where they can access the Internet. However, even some of these courses are semester-based—which means there are starting and ending dates for the courses—while others offer rolling registration and have no beginning or end time (but see the information on financial aid requirements on pages 92–95 before choosing that format). Some distance courses do require in-person registration; others may allow you to print out a form and apply by fax. In some cases this will depend on what larger program you're registered with.

Fast Facts

Guess what—you still may have to prove you've been immunized against childhood diseases, even if you plan never to come within breathing distance of another student or teacher. It may be the law, as in New York:

> Immunization Requirements: As of August 1, 1990, New York State law requires proof of immunity to measles, mumps and rubella. This law applies to all matriculated students taking six or more semester hours who were born on or after January 1, 1957.

Payment

The good news/bad news is that in many online learning situations, you can put the cost of your courses on your credit card—just point and click! Before you do that, however, examine your other options, including scholarships, loans, or direct payment by your employer. Part of your exploration and application process should be a discussion of financial aid or payment plans. Interestingly, cost is one piece of information that even the most helpful of educational sites doesn't put up front on flashing banners—so you'll have to find out about costs carefully. Sallie Mae, the leading financial aid provider for credit students, now makes it psosible for students to pay online (at institutions that sign on for the service) and also provides counseling at a distance. This is another stage at which convenience should be approached with care—and with advice.

Once you've paid, there's another step that's not needed for on-campus learning—a password to get you into the distance education site. Instructions for this should also be clear—and it's when you apply for your password that you find out if all the previous steps have been made correctly! If so, you can begin your course.

Textbooks

There are other nitty-gritty details to even online courses—textbooks, for instance. Yes—remember that print was listed as an important ingredient? While much material can be taken from higher-tech sources, texts are critical parts of most distance programs. However, most college bookstores will willingly ship books to students' homes if they can't come to campus, so you may not even have to come to school to shop.

How do you get your course materials? Here's an example from the Virginia Polytechnic Institute and State University (better known as Virginia Tech):

> Simply click on "Course List" and then "Course Description" and follow the links to your courses. Students will have many options for purchasing texts. Campus informa-

tion or online book store information will be included within the "book info" area under the course description.

In addition, you'll be able—and encouraged—to do research and information gathering via the Web. Each school has guidelines on appropriate use of such material.

Coursework

Okay, so you're set—shine on your virtual shoes, virtual hair slicked back—the ideal virtual student. Now that you're officially a student, you'll have official schoolwork. How to handle the assignments and the homework is covered in the next chapter—but here are some general procedural steps to be aware of before the first day (or night or wee small hours) of class.

Voice of Experience

"Upload an assignment? What does that mean? My first weeks were anxious because I was also a novice at the computer. However, I am proof that it is just not difficult. In fact, I adore online courses because with the computer I can meld life with learning and getting my degrees."

While some programs, both credit and noncredit, long-term or short, are designed and presented by the course provider, many others are created on a virtual framework provided by special services like Blackboard, ed2go.com, or WebCT. In fact, this is becoming a booming business in the world of higher education. These services provide platforms and software as well as guidance to traditional schools and, while they stay behind the scenes, they can be a factor to consider in comparing educational opportunities.

These services are different from providers of canned education; they are more like the architects for a framework to deliver the material. An advantage of these predesigned programs is that they can be easier to navigate than ones put up by those with less experience. The academics may have to learn by trial and error what works and what doesn't, while the technicians have already tried out their system. So sometimes predesigned programs are easier to navigate. In either case, instructions should be clear, especially because instructions are more complex in these venues than "Go to room 447, sit down, pick up your pencil . . ."

Whatever the infrastructure, the most effective courses are, first of all, simple. edCenter, for example, keeps it simple. As this site architect explains on some of the sites it develops, "If you can use a Web browser, you can learn using edCenter. We offer simple learning objects to help you interact with the content and communicate with class members. For example, if you want to ask your instructor a question, you simply click on the Q&A button and type your question. Once the instructor answers that question, the whole class will benefit because the answer will be posted for all students to view."

Each setup will be different, of course—here's an example of the kind of precourse preparation a thorough online provider offers: the World Campus online arm of Penn State University provides checklists so you can determine in advance if you have what you'll need in order to participate in a course. (See the World Campus Technical Requirements page for specific information.) For many programs that have online components, there are even special diagnostics pages where you can test your computer system against program-specific technical requirements!

Once you register for a course, you will be sent a course materials packet that contains the information and resources that you'll need. Packets typically include a welcome letter from your instructor, which describes how to get started with the course, as well as how to contact the instructor; any print materials required for the course, such as a textbook, study guide, and/or readings booklet; and the URL (Web address) for the course home page (if applicable). The packets provide easily accessible information on topics that include:

What will my course be like?

What will my program be like?

How are assignments handled?

How will my learning be assessed?

How will I interact with my instructor and fellow students?

Will I need any special skills to be successful?

as well as information on using online course materials and using academic resources in your courses.

Lest all this be overwhelming, keep in mind that, while it's important to know how to work the technical details of course procedure, most students say that it becomes second nature once they get into the classwork.

Voice of Experience

Ideally, support and information continue throughout your online learning experience. An example:

> Student services are accessible through the UMUC [University of Maryland University College] Web site. Students can apply for admission, search a schedule of classes and check seat availability, order books and materials, search for scholarships and apply for financial aid, and check their financial and academic records. They will also be able to register for courses, pay bills, and participate in financial aid workshops online.

Term papers

Yes, papers, reports, and group assignments are all a part of distance learning programs (just in case you still had any idea that *virtual* meant *magical* or *distant* meant *alone!*). You'll do them the old-fashioned way—researching, writing, and presenting—but, in most high-tech distance courses, you'll do all that research electronically on the Web, collaborating via e-mail or networks; word-process the papers; and e-mail them to your teacher for posting.

Voice of Experience

"It's great to be able to do a paper without ever having to actually go to a library. . . . I got used to being able to correct material till the last minute—but then, it goes right out to the class! Yikes."

You'll have step-by-step guidance for this, too. Here's an example from Penn State:

> *Locating specific on-line resources:* While you are taking a World Campus course, chances are good that you'll want to locate additional information about course topics in order to complete assignments, learn more about difficult concepts, or further explore topics that interest you. If you have access to the Internet, then looking for such resources on-line is a natural! You won't necessarily find everything you are looking for on-line . . . the library is still an incredible resource . . . but sometimes you'll find just what you need."

Today, even most standard library research can be done at a distance online. Many (but not all) university libraries' resources are available electronically, and with a computer and an Internet connection you'll have connections to libraries of other colleges, as well.

Labs

Courses on every topic—including medicine and physical education—are available for credit online from one source or another. However, many programs like those mentioned—or those in nursing or teaching—require hands-on learning or experience for completion. For labs or internships like those, your provider will likely insist that you show up. Perhaps you'll have to make time for an intensive experience on campus—or, if you're closer to the provider, you may have to go on campus one day a week. Learning online is no way to avoid biochemistry—if it's a requirement, you'll still have to pour those chemicals! Some ways that this is handled:

- *Roscoe Hastings of Monroe Community College in Rochester, New York, describes some physical education courses he's designed: Personal Fitness and Fitness Theory and Conditioning. "These are both theory courses designed to help the student understand the value of fitness and how to achieve it," he says. "We started a new program in Golf Management and thought, what better way to provide it than on-line, so we offer Introduction to Golf Management, Golf Shop Operations, The Rules of Golf, Golf Course Maintenance and Golf Internship. These courses are designed to train the person who wishes to seek a career in the golf business. The Internship course requires 135 hours of work at a golf facility . . ."*

- *Sister Teresita Hinnegan and the University of Pennsylvania Nursing School have a program with St. Jude's to train nurse-midwives in very rural areas. Sister Teresita explains that the school can train nurse-midwives at a distance because of on-site professional supervisors who can work with them on the hands-on aspect of the training and exams.*

Researchers observing online and distance learning note that Web-based courses with required labs (in the natural sciences, say, or allied health fields) are often taken by traditional on-campus students who have chosen to take an online course for the sake of its convenience, then simply take their lab courses on campus in the usual way. Students who are truly distance learners must make other arrangements to fulfill their lab requirements. They may spend one or two Saturdays on campus in specially scheduled all-day lab sessions, do their lab work at a local high school or other nearby facility, or run experiments in their home kitchens using a lab kit provided by the college.

Exams

Some tests can be managed online, and some architecture allows for exams to be taken that way too, but, like labs, some tests will have to be completed in person. Increasingly, though, as technology grows more sophisticated and expert providers come onto the learning scene, tests at a distance are possible. ISI, an education provider, explains:

> At appropriate times the instructor tests student retention of the material. Many of ISI's Web-based courses have short online Self-Tests for each unit that students use to evaluate their own progress. Usually an instructor will give mid-term and final exams. But the delivery depends on the school's rules . . . for issuing and proctoring these tests.

Often a distance learner's employer, a local librarian, a Justice of the Peace, or other community members may serve.

As you'll see when you explore many online sites, there are self-tests to evaluate your suitability for distance study, for instance. Your answers are entered electronically and evaluated immediately. Today, courses can also provide exams in the same way.

Training steps

Of course, not all learning is connected to colleges. The preceding process covers academic rules, but the steps related to specialized, noncredit skills training programs are similar—you'll just be dealing with an employer or a training organization instead of a school or college. You may work for an organization that provides a catalog of training programs itself or that encourages employees to get training or advanced education. Or, you may need to sell your boss on the idea of your getting training. This should not be too hard, given the fact that you can be convincing about the ability to get extra training without having to leave your desk or take up office time. In any of these scenarios, you'll need to find a course, find how to sign up for it and pay for it, apply, learn the procedure, and so forth. If it's an online program related to your job, you may without guilt be able to do it on the job; otherwise, it will take time at night, on weekends, or even early in the morning (or how about on a laptop on the commuter train?). In other words, the procedure is similar, even if the provider is not.

Voice of Experience

The master's degree candidate may be sitting at his desk, but he took all his technology management classes while sitting at his office desk, attending classes from his personal computer (PC), viewing lectures via streaming video, and telechatting with his classmates via a telephone bridge. The process is the same; only the setting is different.

Online training is the way people are gaining new skills these days. But there are still other kinds of distance training—perhaps simply cassettes and a workbook, or a videotape run for a group—just not nearly as much going to class. More recently, online training consists of course content delivered via a Web server. Or, it may mean streaming multimedia to users over the Internet. Or, it might be a live chat with streaming audio/video of the instructor and/or students. Books can be presented electronically on the Web. Live streaming communication creates conferencing that mimics in-person training.

Some important caveats

What if your course is not all that you expected?

If you feel you've been treated unfairly by an education provider, you do have some recourse. The government has some say in these matters, for instance. Though the U.S. Department of Education does not approve a school's curriculum, policies, or administrative practices, except as they relate to how the school operates federal student financial aid programs, before permitting a school to participate in the federal student loan programs, the U.S. Department of Education does require the school to be licensed by the state government and approved by a recognized accrediting agency. The state agency that licenses the school, and the accrediting agency that accredits the school, are responsible for monitoring the quality of education and services the school provides.

Here are your options if you're not satisfied with the content provided by a school:

- The court system. *You may want to talk with a lawyer about the possibility of suing the school or others for damages you believe they owe you.*

- State regulators. *You may want to file a complaint against the school with the state licensing agency. (Go to your state's home page and search for the appropriate agency.)*

- The school's accrediting agency. *You may want to file a complaint against the school with the agency that accredited the school. (Go to your state's home page and search for the appropriate agency.)*

You'll find a list of links to trade school accreditors in Appendix D. But avoiding that kind of hassle in the first place is the reason for asking specific questions about accreditation *before* you sign on for an online program. Distance education providers are in such a hurry to impress electronic age students that they may fast-talk their way around the accreditation matter. Saying "XX U has applied for accreditation" is not the same as saying you will get credit for courses you take now!

Heads up on privacy

You're not private in an in-person classroom—why worry about it at a distance? Whether it applies to training or education, privacy *is* an issue. Imagine, for instance, that your employer is training you— or has hired a firm to train you—in new skills. Remember that your employer has access to anything you do or say online, by e-mail, or on tape. This may be easier to image than the wider problem— anything that goes through cyberspace can be accessed at a variety of points that you don't even know about. This doesn't mean you have to be paranoid and reclusive. For some people, this lack of privacy may not feel like a problem at all—it just means you need to be aware of the possibilities. Your personal (and often financial) information is recorded electronically and thus is available electronically to others than those you might intend (for technical details on such privacy protection issues, see Part 6).

Feeling anonymous, you may reveal things about yourself that you wouldn't otherwise. That's fine—but you'll need assurance that your material won't go any further than class.

Voice of Experience

"I really felt comfortable 'talking' to the other members of my class . . . I say things I wouldn't say to people I could see, I think. Of course, with e-mail, it's possible to break that circle of confidence in a snap."

You won't have an option in much of this, because you'll need a password to get into any class that you have paid for—a password that will connect your identifying information to the nonvirtual you. Under privacy laws schools are not allowed to give out information about students—and students are warned about not passing on material to those outside the class. But caution is not a bad idea, anyway. This is just something to keep in mind as you really get into your online learning experience. The next chapter suggests ways to get along now that you've gotten in.

Chapter 13

Working the System

A paradox of online learning is that as far away and isolating as it seems, it can actually be much more personal than face-to-face learning, and that in every form of distance learning, you may need to put more of yourself into the process than you would if you were sitting quietly in a classroom.

Another paradox: in order to deal successfully with other people—students and teachers—you also have to successfully use tools in ways that never applied in a four-walled classroom. In those old days the main tool was a blackboard and chalk. The technology used now is a medium not only for transmitting your education, but also for relating to your peers.

Voice of Experience

Daniel Price, a professor of distance learning at The Union Institute, a leader in all-distance education, describes what it's like:

Recently I "attended" a conference hosted in Hawaii. I attended by way of e-mail, ListServs, and MOOs [multi-user object-oriented environments] and discovered people in Australia, England, and even Oxford, Ohio, some twenty miles away, who are thinking along the same lines and have similar interests and questions. Although some critics of the Internet fear an isolation of learning because of the physical absence of others "going to class," quite the opposite is true. Participants engage in a much wider, even international, circle of learning. Through ListServs today I can "bulletin board" with colleagues on topics of choice. In the future, I will "bulletin board" through sound bites or asynchronous video bites. While personally I prefer the text format as more anonymous, the next generation could be perfectly comfortable with video bites. If they chose, scholars and students could also have simultaneous video conferencing at prearranged times.

Two elements are involved here. One is the tools that make the interaction possible. We began discussing that in Chapter 3. Here you'll find more details on the tools. But perhaps a more important element is the interaction itself. The tips here help you bring the tools, teachers, classmates, and classwork all together, with examples from distance education success stories.

Fast Facts

Does the technology worry you? You're not alone—but it won't last long! Research shows that student attitudes toward technology often improve as familiarity with the technology increases. That is, students new to a particular technology may initially exhibit some concern—usually that means a reluctance to actively participate in the distance classroom. But many studies show that familiarity with technology erodes anxiety and improves participation over time—especially when teachers get involved with help and support.

Tech connections

As you're aware, there are a lot of high-tech tools and systems involved in providing you with a distance education. With just a bit of help, handling even the most sophisticated technologies quickly becomes second nature. There are the old-fashioned tools you'll need to manage—from class participation to quizzes—just in new formats . . . and yes, you do have to hand in homework.

Good schools try to make the system as easy as possible for students, not just by giving them demos of how the system works, but also by administering matters to make everything run smoothly. World Campus sums up the variety of technology that is a matter of course in courses today: "World Campus courses are delivered in a variety of ways. Some courses rely solely on printed materials and utilize surface mail (or fax/e-mail, if accessible to the student) as the means for submitting assignments and interacting with the instructor. Others may require the use of a computer to access course materials, submit course assignments, and interact with the instructor and fellow students . . . and everything in between."

Distance learning experts note that not only does this kind of education require basic access to, and understanding of, workable information systems, including the technology by which instruction is received, but students also often require some form of access to library systems. This might be electronic (and even on-campus students can access many distance libraries electronically), or some other technique needs to be developed and the online searching capabilities of statewide library networks enhanced.

The complexity and cost of setting up these systems explains why high-tech learning isn't cheaper than the in-person version, and why specialists are often called in to manage the new systems. Over the long term, costs and confusion should drop. In the meantime you may need a lot of support. Here are some of the ways this is provided.

First, requirements should be laid out clearly, in advance, as the Virginia Tech intercollege system does:

> Courses utilizing a variety of delivery technologies (hybrid courses) will vary in terms of their specific technology requirements. Depending on the types of technologies used, students may need to download such software as NetMeeting, Symposium, CuSeeMe or other interactive software onto their home computer [*sic*]. Because of the many possibilities, in terms of useable technologies, for every course using a variety of technologies, specific directions will be given on an individual course basis.

In order to handle the media—the means by which you receive your education—the provider of education also provides support systems (usually more complex than chairs and a blackboard). The amount and type of support depends on your system. Even if you're just studying at an extension site, you'll want to be sure your course offers people to provide services at the site and a technician/troubleshooter on hand to fix glitches, as well as such services as access to a fax machine, telephone, and photocopier, to make your studying more convenient.

If you're using interactive video from home or at a special site, you need to be comfortable with a variety of equipment, including computers, videotapes, and visualizers to make demonstrations real. All of this makes it feel as if the instructor is standing right in front of you, and a fax machine allows you to send papers and tests straight in to the instructor. Now, all the technology in the world is not going to make a boring professor less boring. In fact, seeing a boring lecturer via TV (whether streaming or taped) is even more boring, because you're forced to focus only on the teacher's image. At schools that have become aware of this problem, one response has been to try to "Disney-ize" the presentation—to jazz it up almost to the point of entertainment. If that works, fine—but others have tried to train teachers to improve their video presentation, encouraging them not just to stand there but to vary facial expressions, tone of voice, body movements, and eye contact with the camera to enhance communication, and to engage students by using humor, asking questions, and maintaining enthusiasm. Technology actually places more demands on the teachers, as we'll see. And if the teaching continues to be boring—say something! Students have more power these days—and you are entitled to professionalism.

Voice of Experience

A math teacher comments that teaching to a camera takes getting used to. But he's impressed by how producers have jazzed up his business math course, creating a feature that actually shows different terms coming out of the formulas and becoming one. The teacher says this was something he could never do on the blackboard.

When the Internet is part of a distance-delivered course, you may link up with classmates and teachers through Internet and World Wide Web (WWW) access that allows interaction and feedback by computer. To enable participants to get comfortable enough with this to actually learn something, troubleshooting student computer problems needs to become a part of normal instructional responsibilities. You can also expect good distance teachers to build informal training into a class, requiring classroom conferences, electronic bulletin boards, and a minimum number of e-mail communications per week.

All this technology will differ for each course, and is changing and evolving even as you read, so your school will need to explain it to you as much as possible. The point, however, is not the equipment, but how the equipment serves to bring you together with your classmates and your teacher. For instance, if your faculty chooses to be available via electronic mail, Web-based conferencing software, phone, and/or fax to assist with coursework and to answer course-related questions, you need to feel comfortable with that equipment, because although face-to-face teaching is fading fast, effective faculty-student interaction remains key to good learning.

High-class work

Okay, so your computer is cranked up, the videotape is in the machine, or you're sitting looking at a blank TV in a room far away from campus. The technology is in place. Now what?

What's it really like to study at a distance? Student descriptions of the process show that the study activities are really quite similar to what the students were used to—only the details differ. Here's how some providers explain the techniques of managing out-of-class activities and assignments, from completing worksheets and term papers to preparing presentations and portfolios. For each assignment you are given, you'll also receive specific instructions for how that assignment is to be turned in. Ideally, you'll have more than one option for submitting your work—such as a choice between using surface mail or e-mail—so that you can choose the method that best meets your needs. For example, you might surface-mail your term paper or attach it to an e-mail note, or videotape your presentation and send the tape to your instructor, or submit your paper or presentation in the form of a Web page. As sophisticated technology becomes more available in lower-end computers, you may even use streaming techniques for live transmittal of your presentations to your instructor and classmates. (Changing out of your pajamas is probably a good idea for this kind of special event!) After an assignment has been received, it will be graded and the feedback will be shared with you. Since your instructor will be at a distance from you, your response may come via surface mail, e-mail, or an online grade book.

Other features of distance classwork include:

- *Online quizzes that are automatically scored, complete with detailed feedback*

- *Paper-based exams that are taken in the presence of an approved proctor*

- *Course projects that you may work on as part of a collaborative team*

- *Virtual lab experiments that let you manipulate data in order to test hypotheses*

- *Participation in small group discussions that take place online*

- *Self-check (nongraded) activities such as pop quizzes or even crossword puzzles that help you make sure you are comprehending course material*

You can review all your work at any time—and have the special advantage of going back over all notes and class discussions throughout the length of the course, as they all remain either online or on a videotape that you can return to at any time. Likewise, you can redo quizzes and go over lectures repeatedly, so that learning really locks in.

But for all the student-driven nature of this new kind of learning, new patterns that allow you to create your own most effective study habits also make new demands on your self-discipline. Academic research into the nature of distance learning results in observations like these about students' new roles in taking increased responsibility for addressing their own needs:

Distance learners must:

- *Assume greater responsibility for their own learning*

- *Become more active in asking questions and obtaining help*

- *Be respectful of the flexibility required by other students*

- *Be prepared to deal with technical difficulties in the two-way information flow*

Researchers also stress the importance of getting comfortable with these new demands and techniques, because if you don't, learning suffers. At best, unsure students may manage little more than memorization and other "surface" learning—while those who learn to make the best use of new techniques find that learning may be far deeper than in traditional formats. Teachers may be forced to be more organized than behind a messy desk—providing virtual folders where students' work is deposited and assignments are passed back.

Class activities proceed in some familiar fashions, too—but (like it or not) participation is less easy to avoid than in a nonvirtual classroom. Discussions proceed via bulletin boards and chat rooms, and teachers can keep track of who's participating and who's not. But even for those who are usually bashful about joining in, distance learning discussions can be easier to participate in, because you have more time to think. For example, when an assignment has been handed out, you can think about what others have posted to the bulletin board as you click on their messages one by one. When you see a point you'd like to comment on, you click on a Reply button and type in your response, which is then posted to the bulletin board. You continue to read the rest of the messages, replying when you find points of interest.

Voice of Experience

An experienced online trainer notes:

Interestingly, interactions in online courses can sometimes be more in-depth than the face-to-face variety. For one thing, the instructor has more time to reflect on the question and respond with a broader answer so the whole class can benefit.

As the course proceeds, it's likely to follow a pattern like this: each week the instructor assigns units and materials from the course Web site, readings from the textbook and other print materials, paper topics, group projects, and other activities. Students work on their own time, going over the online course material from any personal computer with Web access, whether it's at school, at home, at work, or in the library. They submit completed assignments according to a system agreed upon.

Students and the instructor communicate with each other electronically at least once a week and meet in an online discussion room for each class section if the school does not operate its own conferencing service. In many ways the heart of learning in an asynchronous Web-based course will take place in the online discussion room through threaded discussions on the assigned topics. The teacher can join in or just observe.

Check it Out

Here's how ideas might be shared in an actual class discussion. The teacher posts the question:

Can you think of a way you could use document publishing in the classroom? Would you use it to solve an existing problem or to enhance your existing activities? Post at least two ideas for how you might use document publishing.

1. Go to the "Unit 1 Discussion" forum of our course bulletin board

2. Click on the Compose button to start a new bulletin board posting

3. In the Subject field, type in a meaningful subject line for your posting, one that gives us a hint at your idea

4. Next, type your idea into the large, blank box provided.

5. Click on the Post button to post your message to the bulletin board

6. Finally, review at least two of your peers' postings and provide them with meaningful feedback on their ideas

Teachers find distance discussions help shy people open up, while they also have a better chance of keeping the reins on the occasional talk-hog.

Voice of Experience

"I don't allow any hotdogging by people who take a class just to show off what they know," says an experienced online trainer. "For instance, in my Intro to HTML [Hypertext Markup Language] class, I point out that it's an introductory course and that I and the TAs [teaching assistants] won't comment on any page that doesn't address the assignment."

....

Professorial polish

Polishing the apple has always been the polite way to describe what we (many of us, anyway) do during our school careers to make the teacher smile favorably on us. We might admire his or her outfit or pretend an interest in his or her hobbies. We might go out of our way to ask the right questions after class, or ask the teacher's opinion about something we don't really care about. Smiling at the teacher, raising our hands, and spouting back the same thing that's been poured into us are some other techniques. And it usually works.

But what do you do when you can't even see the teacher, let alone polish his or her apple? Teachers and students alike say the relationship is both the same and different. If you complete the assignments as requested and on time, you're off to a good start; then, the fact that you're at a distance doesn't mean you can't be friendly or ask those special questions. On the other hand, being at a distance doesn't mean you can be rude and get away with it, either!

From the other viewpoint, teachers find they need a new kind of polish themselves. Those who thought distance teaching would be less work and take less time have found—to an even greater extent than the students, it would seem from their comments—that distance teaching takes more work and more time than the in-class kind. And while the goals are the same—to involve students and help them learn for themselves, for instance—some of the techniques are different. In the following text is some of what distance teachers are learning. (Are these efforts going on in your online class?)

Distance teachers find that they have to use effective teaching practices combined with technology to make sure opportunities are included to enhance student interaction by:

- *Planning a block of time for interaction and then letting students know in advance that interaction is anticipated*

- *Initiating an interaction within the first 20 minutes of class to motivate students to participate*

- *Designating students at distant sites to lead discussions or survey the room for questions*

- *Assigning discussion questions in advance of the online or television session*

For audio, computer, or video classes, teachers find these steps effective:

- *Before the class meets, send a welcome letter, course syllabus, relevant course materials, and lists of available resources, contact people, and policies to students.*

- *Send a photo and a short biographical sketch of the instructor to all students. Also, have students exchange photos and biographical sketches.*

- *Conduct a precourse technical training session to discuss the technology and procedures that will be used, whether audio, video, or cyber.*

- *At the first meeting of the class, have students introduce themselves to one another and share background information.*

So you see, you are likely to get to know both teachers and students better at a distance than you might in a standard and largely anonymous class. Here's an example of how one online teacher, Karen Coffey of Monroe Community College in Rochester, New York, presents her distance class and its techniques. It's a great example of the ideal possible from a distance teacher and is clear about what is expected in course learning activities:

For this course there are a variety of learning activities:

1. **Writing Assignments**
   You will write seven essays that ask you to evaluate yourself as a communicator or to demonstrate your understanding of the course material. Each essay carries equal weight and is at least one page but no more than three pages in length.

2. **Discussion of Topics**

   You will actively initiate and participate in these discussions at specific times in the course.

3. **Contribution and Discussion of Shared Resources**

   You will use the Web to collect, analyze, and write about the information that you have gathered. This research will be posted for the class and you will be available to discuss your findings. You will also review the research of classmates and ask questions for clarification or a deeper understanding of their work.

4. **"Try This" Exercises**

   You will practice skills that are presented in a written, nongraded rehearsal for the test and writing assignments.

5. **Rehearsal of Skills**

   You will try out the skills presented in class in your everyday life. This is essential for success on the final demonstration of your skills that are included in your videotaped final interview.

Professor Coffey's expectations for herself and her class:

- Log on according to my log-on schedule.
- Respond to your questions and correct assignments and tests in a timely manner.
- Communicate in a respectful way.
- Help you to understand any information or instructions that you find confusing.
- Treat each of you fairly, which to me means enforcing the rules and guidelines set down for the course in the same manner with everyone.
- Remain positive.

I expect you to do the following:

- Log on at least three times a week.
- Respond to discussion questions within the time frame indicated.

- Turn in or complete all writing assignments and tests when they are due.
- Treat me and others with respect and courtesy.
- Ask me any questions that you have about course readings, information, or instructions.
- Ask our support staff for any technical/systems type of information or assistance.

Professor Coffey's distance instructions are clear—and they also make it clear that this is how we polish the apple: treat the teacher and classmates with respect, and do our work on time! It also helps—especially when we may feel disconnected—to have the course and expectations laid out so clearly.

Professor Coffey goes on: "Let me just say here, in case all of this had a strict tone, that I'm really a nice person who wants you to succeed in this course. I see my role as the person who can help you to achieve the goals that you set for yourself."

See how it comes back to the student? As earlier chapters have recommended, having goals that we set for ourselves is critical to distance learning success.

Here are some of the systems for communication and feedback (using both high and low technology) that distance teachers use to establish and maintain a significant connection with their students:

- Use preclass study questions and advance lesson plans to encourage informed participation by giving students a chance to think ahead.

- Early in the course, require students to use e-mail to contact the teacher and each other—and include keeping an electronic journal as part of the assignments, to help students be comfortable with the process.

- Share work schedules, so students know when to expect feedback. Arrange telephone office hours (including evening hours).

- Use a variety of systems for interaction and feedback, including one-on-one and conference calls, fax, e-mail, video, and computer conferencing—even prestamped post-cards. Be available for in-person visits, too, and contact each student or distance site (or student) every week. For students who don't participate, extra outreach is used.

- Encourage feedback regarding course content, pace, and delivery.

For your part as a student, you have more opportunities to keep in individual, personalized, and private touch with your teacher, since e-mails can be sent 24/7—so all questions can be raised, and comments can flow, in ways they never could in a three-session-per week in-house class.

Similar teacher-student interactions happen in effective training sessions as well. Here's how two distance trainers run their class: They begin with a series of postings to a training site message board, including information about themselves and a general welcome to the class—what learners should expect, how to get the most out of the class and handle homework setting the tone of the class. E-mails come back—an average of 40 per day. Students review their assignments and post questions and comments to the training site message board weekly. The teachers say that feedback and interactivity are the keys to making the online classroom function, and work hard to keep the conversations going.

As a student, what can you expect from your distance teachers by way of response? Research stresses the importance of this interaction, and teachers say they work at it. What actually happens? When you take a course in a traditional face-to-face classroom, you can ask a question of your professor and receive an immediate response. In distance education, with its typical lack of face-to-face interaction, often the responses are not immediate, since instructors are not sitting next to their telephones or computers at all hours. As a distance education student, you simply need to become familiar with your instructor's schedule and availability so that you can know when to expect responses. Getting too pushy about receiving responses will only annoy the teacher. It's important to remember that, although learning is increasingly student focused, the faculty is still the head chef in the learning kitchen. On the other hand, the faculty has a responsibility not only to develop the course content, as in any class, but also to assemble it for distance presentation and to make an effort to connect with "invisible" students. This is definitely a two-way street, but research has shown that good teachers are good teachers, and that they only have trouble at a distance when they let the technology get in the way rather than enhance their presentations.

Experienced distance instructors also know that there are some special challenges that must be met. Since they can't see their students, for example, they miss out on important cues that they are accustomed to responding to, so they must learn to "read personalities in e-mail," as one teacher puts it. They may have to reduce the amount of material they present, because technology can actually add to the work, especially if breakdowns occur. While teachers have always had to prepare in advance, this is actually more true for distance teachers, who must lay out the entire course in advance of the semester. Being aware of faculty challenges like these may help you as a student participate more equally and with more respect in this shared learning experience.

Working with others

Technology is responsible for bringing you together with your classmates as well—and because it takes some extra effort, the result is actually more interaction. Students become less anonymous when the teacher and the class make a special effort to draw everyone in—often in ways that don't happen in general classes.

Who are your classmates and how do you interact? In general, you're likely to find that your classmates are folks who would be less likely than normal to get close, since many distance education students are older and have jobs and families. They must coordinate the different areas of their lives that influence each other—their families, jobs, spare time, and studies. Distance students have a variety of reasons for taking courses. Some are interested in obtaining a degree to qualify for a better job. They tend to be more intent than the average student on getting the most from their courses. Since you may be living in different geographic zones from your classmates (and teacher), that's another element that would ordinarily keep you separate. So working together may become an even greater challenge!

Who are your classmates? One teacher describes a class that might be typical:

> I have had a lot of 20- and 30-year-old female students who work full time, have families and want to go to college. To find a class that fits their schedule is nearly impossible. On-line fits. Another common advantage is child care. Parents would have to find a sitter to come in to watch their kids while they go to school. On-line they put the kids to bed and go to the computer. My students have come from 5 different states. One Kodak worker was transferred to Mexico and completed his class from there.

Your classmates may come from all over the world—or just down the street. How well you choose to know them is up to you: there are some courses where that is worth the effort, and some where you might want to keep private.

In other ways, too, the experience you'll have as a distance student depends largely on what kind of distance study you're involved with. The University of Maryland University College (UMUC) study mentioned earlier observed the activities of distance students in three settings: together at a distant site with a live teacher or with technological delivery; at a distance, using television and conferencing; and at a distance, using computer and Web connections. Here are some of the observations. Does any version sound more appealing to you than another?

On-Site Students' Experience

- Because the faculty member is physically present in the space, on-site students generally have an experience similar to that of the traditional classroom
- May be less tolerant of technological problems and challenges than distant students, because they are unlikely to perceive a personal benefit resulting from the use of technology

Extension Site Students' Experience

- Have flexibility in structuring their time; they are responsible for organizing their work and time to meet course requirements and deadlines
- Must be highly motivated; they need good organizational and time management skills, the ability to communicate in writing, initiative, and a commitment to high standards of achievement

Distant Students' Experience

- Tend to feel somewhat isolated and cut off from the "real" class unless the faculty member makes a concerted effort to include them
- Often form a close working group with students at the same location
- Usually find the mediated experience (even two-way video) to be different from face-to-face communication because the mediation affects perception and communication in some obvious and many subtle ways
- Will make allowances for problems with the technology if they perceive a personal benefit (access to instruction otherwise unavailable; site close to home or work)

Voice of Experience

An online student observes:

Another advantage of taking online courses for me has been the anonymity. A surprising result was that I felt comfortable in sharing some very private information with a group of total strangers. I think, had I had to face these individuals in a classroom setting, I don't think I would have been as open. . . . On the other end of the spectrum, I am a people person. That being said, it would have been nice to talk to classmates and my professors in person. Unfortunately much is missed when delivering your message through the use of technology. There are millions of different physical cues that can help you relate the information you are trying to impart to someone. Human contact also helps people make personal connections and gain support from one another. I know that certain individuals were able to make this connection, but for me, I was so busy that it was really difficult.

· ·

Not surprisingly, the type of distance learning environment you choose has a big impact on how well you do. Other studies have shown that student attitudes about distance learning are frequently linked to components of the distance education experience (like technological breakdowns) rather than generalized about distance learning in total. And, also not surprisingly, the more positive you feel about your role as a distance learner, the more enthusiastic you'll be.

It's also been found that information communicated in ways other than straight lectures seems to be more popular. What seems to work best emphasizes sharing information and working together. UMUC faculty members, for instance, structure conferences around topics, problems, or case studies and assign students to groups to work on projects. Students also form their own online study groups and correspond with each other and their teachers via e-mail. Students and faculty members alike report that the amount and quality of interaction exceeds what they are accustomed to in their classroom-based courses—and that research is wider as well, using Web-accessed databases and full-text retrieval of documents from electronically accessible libraries.

There's also more informal sharing of information through the passing along of downloaded files. One student may have found something on the Web of general interest and can simply e-mail it to his or her classmates. While this needs to be done with some care, due to copyright rules and the college's own rules for use of materials, there does seem to be a trend on the Web of sharing knowledge rather than competing for it. Be that as it may, teachers of many distance classes go out of their way to create group connections, and technology makes it possible to bring students together on networks as well as in chat rooms, so that collaboration on even major projects is a lot easier than when face-to-face meetings must be scheduled. Such collaborations are also more effective, since Web research can be done even as the collaborators "meet."

Need help? Luckily, it's probably more available than are support services on standard campuses (or it should be!)

- Whenever you have a problem, question, or confusion online, e-mail the question or concern! Distance learning tends to move faster than other kinds, so it's easy to fall behind fast if you don't deal with issues right away.

- There's likely a Help button on the home page of your program's learning center. Use it! It provides information on how to navigate the site.

- Broader help about school or program issues is (or should be) available via the computer—if not online help, then a list of office phone numbers that you can bring up on your screen for asking any questions.

If you need general help with your technology, you can turn to the help line of the company that produced it, and while you're waiting in line, you can e-mail your school's tech-help desk. There are plenty of people who can solve your problem simply.

For studying at distance sites, a facilitator or tech aide should be on hand to help with any problems. If not—ask for one!

If you've gotten this far in your online process, you are probably in a program that is supportive. But if your program does not have this kind of help network (and, believe it or not, there are some that simply expect you to jump in without a life jacket!), let your provider know that it's needed . . . or jump ship!

Here's how one class does collaborative learning activities (CLA) or team-based problem solving: three or four students research, analyze, and attempt to solve a realistic problem together. Collaboration can be an effective means for tackling these projects, but achieving this at a distance requires some special efforts. The team gets started by convening in a telephone conference call prior to the start of the CLA to meet the instructor and the other team members. The call sets up the systems that will be used, including strategizing on how best to use communications software and how to divide the work and divide the research. The first chat meeting is likely to consist of e-mailed outlines of the project and initial lists of links to follow up on. Regular meetings are scheduled and drafts of the report are shared using editing software, in preparation for a group presentation that will take place electronically as well. While students are free to study as they like and do research on their own schedules, they do have to be at their keyboards at certain times of the semester.

In Other Words

Online discussion groups or bulletin boards do offer a kind of interaction among yourself, fellow students, and your instructor. They are not live chat, so you do not have to be online at a particular time to participate. You go to the message board and post a comment or question about your assignments or about postings from others. Each school or course may have different formats for its bulletin board system (BBS) or groups, but what they all have in common is the *threaded discussion,* in which the systems group together messages that relate to the same topic. For example, if the instructor posts a message that is titled "Please introduce yourself," then each student's response (the individual self-introductions) would be grouped with the original note. (Definitions of any other term that seems uncertain are in the glossary in Appendix B.)

Do you have to chat? While many teachers and students responding to the survey questionnaire for this book talk of enjoying the chat rooms the most—or of wishing there were more of them—some students find them difficult, and wider reports from the world of distance learning indicate a lack of general interest in them. One teacher reports that though he had hoped that chats would add a personal touch to the courses and would allow him to get to know each of the students, they turned out to be more like an office hour, where students come to ask questions about what will be on an exam.

Many students, it seems, have a hard time getting in on class conversations—and even fewer are happy about having to travel to campus for exams or other events. Distance, they feel, should mean distance, and that is their expectation: to work on their own, asynchronously.

The other way to communicate is by bulletin board or newsgroup. These text-based communication systems enable students and instructors to post and reply to messages placed and read at any time.

Voice of Experience

Online teachers learn that, just as in other classes, they need to control personality clashes and selfish, class-hogging discussions. When someone on the class message board says something provocative and others react hastily, tempers flare and the teacher has to step in to remind the students that the idea is to share knowledge, not fight about it.

So you have your choice to keep your distance from your fellow students or to get chummy. But any kind of distance communication does seem to make it easier for students of all types to participate in class. And all distance communication calls for one skill that's unique to high-tech education.

Netiquette brings it all together

Classmates, homework, and teachers all require netiquette. This is one aspect of learning that is indeed different from the in-class experience—and mastering it is critical to your success, because even though you're talking online via e-mail at some distance, your manner of speaking can be easily read. Some would say that tone of voice is easier to pick up online than in person.

In the old days, a schoolchild might be graded on conduct. These days, conduct shows through e-mail, BBS, and chat room communications, so following the netiquette rules that govern online communication matters to your classmates and is one key way to impress your teacher and probably affect your grade.

These guidelines are based on common sense and basic courtesy, but, again, technology makes a difference in how they work. Just as you (probably) wouldn't stand up on your chair in class and yell at everyone, so you don't "shout"—that is, use all capital letters—in e-mails. There are lots of other rules for this new form of communication, including the following:

- *Make messages short and to the point.*

- *Use a meaningful subject line, so that your readers and recipients have a clear idea of what the message contains. Examples: rather than "Comment" in the subject line of the e-mail or posting, type "Feedback on Jane's ornithology notes."*

- *Identify yourself. Some courses have their own Web-based e-mail, so all participants know you and the topic. When using personal e-mail, however, be sure to identify the course you're referring to. Also, include your signature at the bottom of your messages. This footer can be added automatically by adjusting the preferences in your e-mail program. It should include your full name and any contact information—address, phone, fax—you wish to share.*

- *Take care in emphasizing words: use all caps sparingly—only to highlight an important point or to note a title or heading. Asterisks around a word make a strong point without reverting to shouting.*

- *Be thoughtful and cautious in what you say, especially about others. Remember that electronic messages are easily forwarded. A good rule of thumb: don't say anything you wouldn't want to see quoted in the newspaper!*

- *When responding to someone else's message, focus on ideas, not the person. Antagonistic messages are called* flames, *and flaming someone is not cool. Would you call that person that name in a face-to-face talk? Then don't do it at a distance!*

- *Show respect for other opinions, especially keeping in mind that the Internet brings people together from around the world and that we don't all share the same views or background.*

- *Be careful when using sarcasm and humor. It doesn't come across as it does in face-to-face communications, and jokes are easily misunderstood as attacks. Label jokes as <joke> or*

<not>, or use emoticons—tiny pictures made from ordinary ASCII characters intended to be looked at with your head tilted to the side that can be used to add a personal touch to your messages.

- *Don't use obscenities in your messages. You never know who you might offend, and it makes you look tacky (remember, those messages stay put or get passed on!). To express yourself fully as needed, use a mixture of ASCII characters like "@#%$" instead of the real thing.*

- *Don't overuse acronyms. Acronyms—the initial letters of words—can be handy, but you can overdo them. Messages too full of acronyms can be confusing and annoying to the reader. Some good ones include:*

IMHO = in my humble/honest opinion

FYI = for your information

BTW = by the way

- *Be careful not to get too personal too fast. Electronic communications environments can quickly get to feel intimate. As if you were talking in the dark, or by candlelight, you can be tempted to share your life story with someone you know only through some distant exchanges.*

- *Don't forward messages without asking first! This is considered extremely rude—but remember that it happens, so choose your own words with care, remembering that they might be shared with the universe. (Remember, too, the points about protecting your privacy.)*

- *Be aware of potential compatibility problems when passing on electronic files. If recipients' systems are not compatible, they may not be able to open attachments. Ask first, and whenever possible, paste in messages rather than attaching them (unless they're very long). Check to see that the message prints out properly at the other end, since screen layouts differ, too. Be clear about who you are and what you're attaching! Computer viruses are often spread through attachments, so recipients may be very cautious about opening them unless they know they are legitimate.*

- *Beware of sharing copyrighted materials. Not everything on the Internet is cleared for fair use. Much of it belongs to someone else—the writer or other creator. Ask for guidelines about what is okay to use and how to use material that is protected by copyright.*

- *Finally, schools and classes may have their own individual netiquette rules as well, such as not sending commercial pitches or chain mail to your classmates. It is important to follow the guidelines in order to be part of the virtual group!*

How are we doing?

Distance teachers are encouraged to have their students evaluate programs. You can too. Here are the items that count most in distance programs. How does yours stack up? If there are any areas that could be strengthened, you can raise the issue (politely!) with your teacher or the class. Points to consider:

Is course delivery easy to access and understand?

Are assignments appropriate?

Is content clear?

Is class time well spent?

Could the teacher be more effective? How?

How might the course be improved?

Here is another way of evaluating the class. Teachers might ask you to do this at some point toward the end of the class; but such evaluations should be anonymous unless you already have your grade!

List five weaknesses of the course.

List five strengths of the course.

If you were teaching the course, what would you do differently?

What did you think would be covered in this course but was not?

Would you recommend this course to a friend? Why or why not?

Consider the following areas and rate them:

Use of technology—ease concerns, problems, positive aspects, attitude

Class formats—effectiveness of type (lecture, discussion, question and answer, group); quality of questions or problems raised in class; openness for students to express themselves

Class atmosphere—supportiveness of student learning

Quantity and quality of interaction with teacher and classmates

Course content—relevance, knowledge, organization

Assignments—usefulness, appropriate level, timeliness of feedback

Tests—frequency, relevance, preparation, feedback

Support services—useful facilitator, technology, library services, instructor availability

Instructor—contribution as discussion leader, organization, skill at maintaining class balance, preparation, positive attitude, openness to student views

Do you see how similar the rating points for an effective distance learning experience are to those you'd use for traditional education? That's the point: there are special electronic skills you may need, but those are learned quickly. The rest is about dealing with knowledge and with people. And, as in old-fashioned school, the key player in learning is you. That's the simple focus of the next chapter.

Chapter 14
Getting a Grip

The previous "how-to" chapters have focused on the tools and the people you need to deal with in your distance learning (DL) ventures. This one hits the bottom line—you. It may not sound like a big deal, especially when you consider that all it really takes to develop good online study habits and work independently for success is the ability to manage your time and to work by the rules. Simple-sounding? Yes. But easy? Not always. First, given the fact that one of the main reasons people cite for taking a distance education course or program is a busy schedule, you get a clue as to why fitting yet another piece into that busy schedule can be tricky.

Just as education is increasingly student driven, so your own life as a student is not, increasingly, in your own hands. While distance students can be free from that 8 A.M. language class, or the demanding training course coming at the end of a strenuous workday, they now need to take responsibility for arranging their own study schedules. This requires a level of commitment and a skill at organization that become important new study skills in themselves.

Since problems with self-organization are among the leading causes (along with technical difficulties or disappointment with content) for dropping or even failing online courses, they need to be addressed and corrected before the whole effort becomes a waste of time and money.

Managing yourself

It's been noted that online or distance learning can actually be more demanding than classroom study. One reason is that you're much more on your own. How do you get up, get going, and get organized?

You may be feeling excited and eager about this new experience, and the self-tests you took back in chapter 6 may depict someone who's suited to this learning style. Nevertheless, before you hook up with a full-fledged distance program, take one more look. What are you planning as the result of this learning experience? Time management is not really effective when it's no more than juggling a lot of miscellaneous tasks. Rather, it takes being goal-directed: you have to feel a clear purpose to your busyness.

So now's the time to review your goals. Go back to the self-tests in Part 3. Put them on the fridge or the bathroom mirror or the computer screen (or all three). Why was it, exactly, that you decided to study online instead of in class? Now that you know it's not cheaper, quicker, or easier, ask yourself the following question:

My need to take a distance course is:

1. High—I need it immediately for a certificate or job or other important reason.

2. Moderate—I could take a substitute or an on-campus class.

3. Low—I'd just like to try it, and everybody's studying that way.

The greater your need for online study, the greater your likelihood of succeeding at the course—so answer honestly!

At a more fundamental level, how much time do you actually have available for study? Spend a week or so keeping an honest tally of the hours you already spend, and note when you seem to have the most time in one slot. Is there a pattern? Ask yourself the following questions:

My current schedule is:

1. Predictable—I can count on being able to plan, well in advance, blocks of time that I can devote to schoolwork.

2. Uneven—sometimes last-minute meetings or events come up, and I'm stuck.

3. Nuts—I rarely know when I'm going to have free time that I can spend on classwork.

Considering my professional and personal schedule, the amount of time I have to work on an online course is:

1. Seven to nine hours per week.
2. Four to six hours per week.
3. One to three hours per week.

Even the largest of those amounts is not enough, according to distance learning experts. Here's how they figure it: The amount of time that you'll spend on a distance course is about the same as the amount you need for a campus-based course. A common formula for a traditional course looks like this:

Start with the total number of hours spent in class
Add 3 hours for every 1 hour spent in class
= Total amount of time devoted to course

For instance: you are taking an on-campus course that meets three times a week, an hour each time, for 15 weeks. To the three hours a week of class, add the amount of time you need outside of class to complete assignments, read, and study—that is, an additional nine hours a week (3 × 3). Your total time spent on the course each week, then, will be somewhere around 12 hours.

Time spent in class:	3 hours
Time spent outside of class:	9 hours (3 × 3)
Total amount of time:	12 hours per week

That same three-credit, 15-week course via distance learning will demand the same 12 hours per week, or 180 hours per semester.

Voice of Experience These two distance students had to drop out: he juggles a full-time job, his classes, and helping to care for his young child; she is trying to work toward her degree while raising three children, who are all under the age of 7. She also runs a day care center for six preschoolers in her home. No way do they have 12 hours a week to spare for even one course!

Got time?

Can you make more time? Probably. There are 168 hours in a week (10,080 minutes!) for you to use in any way you choose. If it seems like you don't have enough time to get everything done, it's probably because you're not using the time you do have as effectively as you could. All it takes is a little organization and a plan that fits your goals and needs.

Individuals have their own approaches to organizing their lives—and if your self-tests showed that this wasn't your most comfortable skill, your studying may take longer than you expect.

Make your own time-flow scheme by calculating how much time you spend:

> Working
> Commuting
> Doing domestic chores
> Traveling
> Attending to personal matters
> Sleeping/exercising
> Doing recreational activities
> Leaving this many hours: _____

If a typical course takes 12 hours a week, how many courses can you, in reality, manage? Sure, you can do your coursework at four in the morning, if you can be awake—but it's still going to require 12 hours a week. So, if your schedule is tight, it's best to try out one course before enrolling in a whole program.

The freedom of online learning has great appeal—but remember that, although you can schedule your own learning times, you still have to make time for learning. Students who've had success in this area say that they approach their distance education scheduling as they would any other old-fashioned class:

- *Get out a calendar or open your software calendar on the screen. For each class, note any required get-together times as well as labs or exams.*

- *Note your schedule for other aspects of your life, and commit yourself (in writing, on your calendar) to doing the work at a certain time. Even if that time is 2 A.M., that is when you attend class.*

- *If the only time you have is in odd moments, try to avoid classes with required chats.*

- *Squeeze the day. Find time to study late at night, while commuting, or at work.*

What are you prepared to give up to make time? And, have you calculated in enough flexibility so that if you need to go to a library to log on to the Internet or to an interactive visual communications (IVC) or other distance site to participate, you have added that time allotment into your schedule? Don't forget that you'll have to arrange it so you can be there when the faculty is there.

There's nothing magic about distance education. Why do people do it? Here are some firsthand explanations from students in various programs surveyed:

Did it take more or less time?

Took less time because I had no commute. Also, I could break up my sessions in smaller slots, rather than sit for several hours.

What special techniques do you need to organize time?

This works best for self-disciplined people.

Would you sign on for this kind of online/distance program again?

Yes, I would do the whole program this way if I could.

Efficient studying

Studying for distance classes is, like so much else in this kind of education, the same but different. You get assignments and have to complete them by a given time; you work with others on projects; you write reports and take tests. Since (if you're like many distance students) your schedule is probably already quite full, you'll want to make your studying as efficient as possible. Experts on studying describe this pattern for effective learning—whether for a home-work assignment, an exam, or a semester-long course: "preview—view—review."

> Preview: in deciding your plan, first preview the entire course—it should be laid out for you ahead of time, just as a syllabus describes a traditional course. Plan ahead for reports, papers, exams, and chatroom hours.

> View: do the work—and it's especially important, other students say, to keep up with it. The temptation is to goof off, but catching up at a distance is harder than in a classroom.

> Review: be sure you have all the materials and notes. (Your notes and all the class discussions as well as the lectures are easy to find, since they stay on the site for the entire course.)

Note that this pattern works on tests—you'll do well to get an overview of the questions, do the test, and then go back and check your answers. It's also good for reading any texts: glance over a whole chapter, read it, and go back over it.

That formula is fine for getting through a course when you're busy. But if you want to really get the most out of a course, educational experts compare the surface with the in-depth approach. Many distance students are so busy—and perhaps so overwhelmed by dealing with technology—that they take only this surface approach:

> Focus on the text or instruction itself.
>
> Focus on discrete elements rather than the whole picture.
>
> Memorize facts and formulas for tests.
>
> Use tricks to connect concepts and facts.

Treat assignments as something imposed by the instructor.

View class as assignments and tasks cut off from everyday reality.

Distance professors see a need for students to become more selective and focused in their learning in order not only to master new information but to absorb material that is of value. This requires the deep approach:

Focus on the meaning of the teacher's offerings.

Connect new ideas to previous knowledge.

Relate class facts to real experience.

While distance education with its techno-razzle-dazzle might seem to encourage the surface approach, it can actually allow for a deep approach because of the opportunity for thought allowed by distance postings and the varied backgrounds and opinions that virtual classrooms attract. So, unless speed is a necessity for some reason, you might want to think in terms of getting the most out of one or a few classes instead of taking as many as you can force into your schedule.

Voice of Experience

More from the survey of distance learners:

What tips can you offer others on how to succeed as an online student?

Interact in chat sessions, keep in touch with professor and team members via email. Do class readings regularly and do not fall behind.

Is it more demanding or less so than traditional classes?

Some classes ARE more demanding—but also more rewarding.

In what way(s)?

The professor gets to know each student. In my case as a student, there is no chance he/she will miss out on what is on my mind, what my answers are, what my class input is, how much I do or don't know. I love it!

Students can all look at the same material at the same time for one thing. And any class discussion or teacher lectures stay on your site indefinitely, making it easier to go back over your notes. It's also easier to add to a discussion: in a classroom, once your opportunity to speak has passed, it's too late. In high-tech classrooms, input is possible continuously—so if you wake up in the middle of the night with a brilliant idea, you can contribute it.

Voice of Experience

The Union Institute, an experienced provider of college courses at a distance, tells it like it is:

Are online courses easier somehow?

Not really. Just because a class is online doesn't mean you get off easy. In fact, our learners tell us that the personal interaction with professors and other learners makes the learning experience so intense—tremendously practical and thoroughly enjoyable—that they often do more than the minimum required work.

It's up to you

Time management requires care. Self-management requires even more! One common theme that runs through all the input from students, teachers, and researchers relates to students' (that's you) responsibilities for managing their own education.

Here are some of the observations:

> I think on-line classes have some strong features. The first is that students are completely on their own as far as how much they want to learn. In the classroom many good students are held back by students with less ability or motivation. On-line there is no disruption or restriction for the serious student.
>
> A student can sign on at any hour of the day or night, taking part at times that best fit his or her schedule. While

this flexibility is unprecedented, it requires greater than average discipline and does not allow a student to "coast." Students devote an average of fifteen to twenty hours a week to their studies.

Plan how you will manage your time. Good time-management skills and the ability to set and follow priorities are two very important skills for success in an online course.

Don't feel that all the work must be done at the computer. You may find it helpful to download or print out pages so that you can refer to them at other times or work away from the computer.

Look for alternate ways of handling the course in case of a computer breakdown or other problem. For instance, would you be able to access another computer (such as by using a friend's or going to a computer lab) if there is a problem with your computer or your ISP [Internet service provider]? Ask the instructor for tips that may apply specifically to the course.

What tips can you offer others on how to succeed as an online student?

Get a good phone connection and use your search engines, and much material can be found to help with assignments. For chat sessions, it helps to have read the next assignment, even though it is a day before that assignment period begins.

> I didn't even know how to log onto the Internet. So I had my son sit with me the first couple of times to help walk me through it.

Attitude matters

A positive attitude is important to success in any field, and in scholastic work it certainly counts for a lot. In distance learning, it counts for even more, according to the Center for the Study of Distance Learning:

Attitude toward learning is an important factor in eventual academic success. Research data on student attitudes toward distance learning can be grouped into four categories: attitude toward the technology, attitude toward distance education teaching methods, attitude toward student and teacher interaction, and attitude toward being a remote student.

The last point, the researchers note, is especially important, because, despite all the convenience and high motivation of distance learning, if students don't believe they can learn a lot at a distance, they won't. It's also important to note that the Center reports that those who have taken distance courses have generally responded positively to the experience and would recommend it to other students. In other words, if you expect to learn a lot from a distance course, you are more likely to. But you'll also need to expect to participate in some new ways.

William Draves, director of the Learning Resource Network, sums up the advantages and the responsibilities of students in online programs:

A learner can learn at her or his own speed. With traditional classes, a learner has one chance to hear a concept, technique or piece of knowledge. With online learning, a learner can replay a portion of audio, reread a unit, review a video, and retest him or herself.

A learner can focus on specific content areas. With traditional classes, each content area is covered and given the relative amount of emphasis and time that the teacher deems appropriate. But in a ten unit course, a given learner will not need to focus on each unit equally. For each of us, there will be some units we know already and some where we have little knowledge. With online learning, we as learners can focus more time, attention and energy on those units, modules or sections of the course where we need the most help and learning.

A learner can test himself daily. With online learning, a learner can take quizzes and tests easily, instantly receiving the results and finding out how well she or he is doing in a course.

The interactivity and responsibility demanded in online study are the hallmarks of the kind of active learning that many educators feel has optimum results. The responsibility extends to some more fundamental matters as well. For instance, students also need to take their own steps to be sure their education is on track. Following are some student suggestions based on actual experiences:

> I feel it's imperative that there is a timely manner to receive correspondence about the course. E-mail is probably the best way to do this. I have had instructors who wanted things to be mailed (US Postal Service), but for some students this is a problem (where I am it takes 2 to 3 weeks to get or send mail to the East Coast!). So I had to speak up—distance is supposed to be "distance."

> "Make contacts": I think in my case the DL program was in a growing phase, and I could see it getting more refined as time went on. Overall I was pleased, but it was also beneficial to get to know a few key individuals in the DL program, and be able to email or call them if there was some sort of administrative problem.

If the student is having problems or questions, it's his or her own responsibility to point them out, because otherwise nobody knows about them! For instance, at a remote learning site, students have to report to the instructor any technical problems they are having. If the instructor cannot alleviate the problem, he or she will notify the on-site coordinator. Common technical problems that could occur include:

Can't hear the instructor/fellow students

Can't read what the instructor is writing

Can't read presentation material—too small, text coloring doesn't show up against background, too much text on one slide

Can't see the instructor (not switching the camera enough)

Material is out of focus

Video/audio problem

What if you're studying online and the computer goes down? The education provider will have advice about this and will offer a backup system of some sort—but you also may need to back up your own system; have a "Plan B"—maybe a borrowed computer to go to in case of a crash.

You're also entitled (and expected) to actively communicate with the instructor throughout the course regarding the course content, classroom procedures, and technical problems.

Some instructors would compel students to participate in class meetings to discuss their progress, but others insist on freedom: an asynchronous Internet class is the best way for them.

Summing up the bottom line for organizing one's time and oneself, one student simply says: "It requires a lot of self-discipline!"

Summing it up

So you want to be a distance student. You've set your goals and explored your options. You've tested out possible sites and signed on for one course. You know how many hours you have to spend on studies, and you're determined to proceed. You've finally gotten all the high-tech details down to a level of comfortability. What now?

When we enumerate the key steps to take, they don't sound too high-tech, but they're what all the students and teachers report as important:

- *Manage your time.*
- *Plan ahead.*
- *Pay attention and keep in touch!*

We will discuss more about what makes for online success in the next chapter.

Chapter 15
Making That A

Preview—view—review: that's the pattern for successful distance study, as well as for successfully learning anything. Now this book is at the review stage, so we'll look back and restate some of the key points in becoming a successful online student. Another way of putting it that is more familiar to those in management or service professions is ADIE (or APIE), which stands for Assess, Design (or Plan), Implement, Evaluate. Any project you're involved with—including achieving success in distance learning—can succeed with this series of steps:

Assess—in this case, ask: what do I need as an education? What schools are good for me?

Plan (or Design)—figure out how to optimize the distance education experience.

Implement—start the program, and pay attention.

Evaluate—ask: is it what I expected? What needs changing? Go back and reassess, and start the process again.

Characteristic of the APIE design for planning is that it's fluid: you never stop. When you get to the evaluation stage, you go back to assessment. That's an important message to remember when you're considering new forms of education: no matter what you choose, based on what you've learned and observed, you can change, with little adjustments or big new moves. First, review what this book has covered so far:

- *What is online study?*
  - ★ *The types of distance learning*
  - ★ *How the types of distance learning work*
  - ★ *Who provides distance learning?*

From what you've learned here, do you have a clear idea of the possibilities offered by distance learning, as well as the myths? Have you checked the Web sites of providers and of resources to discover more details? (see Part 7).

- *Is distance learning for you?*
  - ★ *What's in line for you?*
  - ★ *Success scan*

From what you've learned, what are the most likely possibilities to meet your needs?

- *How to choose a distance education provider*
  - ★ *The steps to take*
  - ★ *What to look for*

Use this section as a handbook to walk you through the process of picking a virtual school.

The section covering the "bigger picture" can put your experience into a useful context from the teacher's, the trainer's, and your own future perspective.

- *The Bigger Picture*
  - ★ *Teacher's Spot*
  - ★ *Re: Training*
  - ★ *Looking Ahead*

- *How to Succeed at a distance*
  - ★ *Following procedure*
  - ★ *Working the system*
  - ★ *Getting a grip*

Have you gotten the idea that success in the virtual classroom involves some very down-to-earth steps?

Finally, review the self tests to personalize this process:

What's best for me? Jot down a word or two about the optimum type of distance education that seems most comfortable.

Which provider will fit my goals? Note the goals and the kind of provider most likely to get you there.

Making my match. Which providers have you picked? Or check the links in Appendix D for more choices. And remember that the decision is not final . . . ever!

As you start your program of study, pay attention to what you're getting out of it. If it's not quite what you'd expected, you may want to change providers—but you may want to be sure that it's not you who's not quite hitting the mark. That's what the rest of this chapter is about.

Quick study

What is the best way to study? Preview—view—review.

Preview—get an idea of what you're going to learn (or what's on a test).

View—go through the material or the test questions carefully.

Review—go back over the information to seal in what you've learned (or make sure you've answered the questions right).

APIE applies here too: *assess* what the course is going to be like; *plan* how you're going to accomplish what's needed; take action to *implement* your plan and follow the instructions; and *evaluate* how you're doing (the teacher's test will do that, too—but you should know for yourself how you're doing).

Good distance education courses are set up so that you can follow this pattern: they'll tell you what the learning objective is and then encourage you to take an overview of how you'll get there. And, just as successful students in a standard course look over the course outline and at least flip through the texts in advance, so can you on most online and many distance learning classes.

One edge on success in high-tech classes is that all the information is still there for you to go back over as you move along in the course. Good students know to review their notes throughout the semester—but having the real thing there is more vivid and more accurate than the reviewing of your own notes. Then do the work as you go along—even at a distance, teachers (and your classmates) know when you've been looking on or not participating, and you'll have to keep up with the quizzes and papers just as in standard courses. Another example: in order to get as much out of this book as possible, you've not just skimmed the contents, but worked the self-tests as you've gone along, stage by stage. And while there will be no final exam here, this is the place where you can review and get ready for the next stage of your online learning adventure.

Distance learning tests are often not like standard exams, but they'll give you the opportunity to review what you've learned. Will you get an A? Maybe, but acing tests is not the main point in education anymore. Anyone who can memorize can get an A. The new learning media—whether computers or multimedia—are dynamic, and the education they offer is dynamic, too. It's about more than getting the answers right. It's the process that's more important—and sticking with it.

Keeping score

When we ask the experienced and the experts what characteristics predict a student's success at distance, we get answers like these:

Hamline University, St. Paul, Minnesota, offers these observations about success: "Our courses are very interactive, so in order for them to work well, the students need to be willing to share their expertise, their experiences, their questions and their thinking with one another. Students who are passive and just expect to be instructed will not benefit as much from such a class as those who are willing to take responsibility for their own learning."

More formally, the Center for Distance Learning Research has come up with these factors influencing student learning outcomes in distance education: "The demographic and psycho-social characteristics of distance education participants interact to influence satisfaction, achievement, and persistence in their learning activities." The Center found that factors influencing satisfaction include a need for control and autonomy, learning styles, perception of social presence, and levels of interaction. It's been found that a combination of motivation, use of a variety of learning strategies, and a preference for visual learning was most predictive of achievement. Persistence also seems key in distance learning success. It's demonstrated by completion of courses, programs, or degrees, and is a broader measure of student success. Self-confidence is an excellent predictor of persistence. And what enhances the self confidence that creates the persistence that leads to success? Instructor empathy, successful progress toward an educational goal, and increasing familiarity with distance learning. On the other hand, self-confidence, persistence, and success are undermined by factors that include unfamiliarity with distance education, skills deficiencies, and overcommitment of time and energy due to inexperience or insufficient counseling. Further, students who receive support from friends, family, and employers are found to be more successful in integrating academic and environmental responsibilities and are more likely to persist than are those who do not receive such support. These students need to be perceived as self-directed, yet concurrently experience legitimate dependency needs for approval, support, and leadership in unfamiliar activities. If adult students, especially, are not supported in psychologically balancing these conflicting needs, they are less likely to persist and more likely to give up.

In sum: persistence, and all that goes into it, combined with interaction, multimedia formats, and active movement add up to make for success online. How do you and your educational programs stack up? Some things you can change: if you feel a need for more support, either from your network or the school's, for example, you can seek it. Also, if you're feeling shaky about technology or class relationships, or simply about going back to school, take comfort in knowing you're not alone—many students feel that way. Nervousness shouldn't make you give up ahead of time, and support should be there when you need it to get started.

Increasing numbers of schools are understanding distance students' special needs and finding ways to meet those needs, including needs for advising, access, communication, and administrative assistance. Advising and counseling often require attention to issues unique to distance learners, including their overcommitment to a wide variety of life demands.

Let's review some distance study facts:

1. Distance study students can sometimes end up neglecting their coursework because of personal or professional circumstances, unless they have compelling reasons for taking a course.

2. Some students prefer the independence of distance study; others find it uncomfortable.

3. Distance study gives students greater freedom of scheduling, but it can require more self-discipline than on-campus classes.

4. Some people learn best by interacting with other students and with instructors, but distance study does not provide much opportunity for this interaction.

5. Distance study requires students to work from written directions without face-to-face instructions.

6. It may take as long as two weeks for distance students to get comments back by mail from their instructor.

7. Distance study requires at least as much time as on-campus courses—and in many instances up to three times more.

8. Distance study frequently uses technology for teaching and communication.

9. Printed materials are the primary source of directions and information in distance study.

10. Distance study classes often require written assignments and projects.

Other studies describe successful distance students as having motivation, planning ability, and the ability to analyze and apply the information being taught. Professor Roscoe Hastings of Monroe Community College, Rochester, New York, observes: "Student success on-line is really no different than in the classroom. Those who apply themselves and are truly interested in learning will be very successful. Those striving to achieve a grade will demonstrate that and be moderately successful. They will usually select projects or topics that they can find lots of information on easily, whereas the learner chooses a topic that has personal interest or value. Students who are not really sure why they are in college usually don't perform very well, usually as a result of not doing their work on time."

Putting all of this simply, Claudette, a 55-year-old retiree who is a highly successful distance student with the Union Institute's program, says, "What you need is goals and focus."

Tips for success

So how do you pull it all together? Some of the leading online education programs offer their students and potential students guidelines for success. For instance, VT online, from Virginia Tech, notes that students who actively cultivate strategies to ensure their success flourish in a distance learning environment.

Summing up, students who succeed in distance learning:

- *Are actively involved in their learning*
- *Can focus on their goals*
- *Prioritize their responsibilities*
- *Reach out for the assistance they need*
- *Pay at least some attention to their health and wellness*

For specific information regarding such topics as study skills, time management, test anxiety, relaxation techniques, and other wellness-related issues, try the following Web site:

http://www.ucc.vt.edu/stdyhlp.html

It's the kind of student service that more distance programs need to provide.

The University of Wisconsin's extension program provides these study tips for success:

Become An Effective Distance Learner

First, you need the right tools. Will you need a VCR? Access to a fax machine? Does your computer have adequate hard-drive space? Is your connection to the Internet reliable? Home computers are a must for most distance courses.

Communication Skills

If you're taking an online course, practice posting to a bulletin board. If you'll need to speak into a microphone, develop your speaking skills. Remember that organization, grammar and the appropriate style are important in whichever medium you choose.

Here is a once-over of some tangible practicalities to keep in mind: you will want to have moderate experience with using a computer so that you will be comfortable using all of the soft-ware and hardware required for the course. You will need to know how to enter and retrieve information on the computer in order to be able to receive and submit assignments and other course materials. Other useful skills include the ability to use a word processing program; the ability to send and receive e-mail (including the use of attachments); and knowing how to download files, as well as a good understanding of the World Wide Web and its use—enough so that you are able to navigate from one site to another, to find things on the Web, and to do searches if they are part of an assignment. And if you need help with any of this, you need to be able to find it, preferably from your course provider.

You will need at least a computer, a modem, and a connection to the Internet, which you get from an Internet Service Provider, listed in the phone book (unless your school has a suggestion). The more up-to-date and faster your equipment is, the better—but, if you don't have this equipment right now, you should be able to access it at your school or library. In any case, you'll want a backup in case your computer goes down.

Though you needn't be a computer expert, you should have enough experience with using computers and software so that you will be able to figure out how to use programs that are new to you, in case you are only able to receive basic help. A supportive school should provide you with more than basic help along with the communications software that is handed out.

Voice of Experience

"I had had almost no experience with computers before, but I am on the Dean's List and should be graduating with honors, basically because of online courses."

Summing up some of the observations made throughout the book: your chances of success with an online course are higher if:

- *You have a strong need or reason to take the course. That need can help you get through difficult times, such as busy schedules.*

- *You do not find independence uncomfortable and will not miss being with others in a classroom.*

- *You are able to discipline yourself to work at the course regularly and keep up with the deadlines.*

- *You are able to learn well by doing the required work on your own, without depending on interaction with other students as a means of learning.*

- *You are able to read and to figure out what to do by yourself, rather than depending on hearing instructions.*

- *You do not expect the course to be easier than, or require less time than, a classroom course.*

- *You do not find it difficult to communicate with the instructor to ask for help or clarification.*

More user tips

Take the time to become familiar with using the World Wide Web and e-mail, if you are not already experienced with them. Also, make sure that you understand how to get around in the course, as well as how to use the computer and all appropriate software. If you have any questions or are unsure about how to begin, ask the instructor right away, to avoid getting behind in class.

"The biggest challenge in taking these courses is the fact that you don't have direct contact on a regular basis with your instructor," says a student. "You have to be the type of person who is comfortable and confident in your work, because the feedback is not immediate."

Here are the steps to take to find the online learning most likely to add up to success for you:

- Gather information about distance learning, about yourself, and about the possibilities.
- Explore the possibilities of the kinds of courses and providers.
- Check out the facts—ask good questions before you decide, especially about specifics on the kinds of distance learning actually offered.
- Set goals for yourself and your education.
- Choose a program.
- Set a course for success: plan your study time, and stick with your plan.
- Keep asking questions in class, about class, about your goals, etc.
- Follow suggestions and head for success.

How will you know if you are a success? (1) If you reach your goal and still find it a worthwhile goal, and (2) if you're still learning something, no matter what!

Summing up success

Cathryn Scheid, a Hamline University student, became a believer in online work: "I followed Hamline University's outline of required courses, but the order in which I finish this degree will be determined by which courses are taught online and when." Judy Rowe also went back to school, online, at University of Maryland University College (UMUC), and says, "YES," her distance education experience was better than expected! "I suggest a student enter an online course with an open mind and an open heart," Judy says. "Online learning has been the most fulfilling experience of my academic learning. One may choose to sit and listen, or pour out one's cognitive, emotional, and spiritual philosophies. I say we have finally found a better mousetrap, and the world should beat a path to our door."

The last word on success

By now, millions of students have made their way through distance education—many of them via institutions that weren't necessarily so big in the old world of education, but that have the student in mind. As we've said, that's the key to finding a course that works for you. From one of those providers we borrow the last word in how to succeed online. This acronym from Virginia Tech sums up what you'll need:

Start right away
Understand your course requirements and expectations
Communicate with your instructor
Check and follow course deadlines
Expect to succeed
Seek help if you have a question
Stop procrastinating

Success? Yes! But you're not done yet (remember APIE?): restart your online success search with the extensive lists in the section that follows. But first, fill in the blanks on this personalized study plan.

Personalized Study Plan

Goals: _____   By deadline: _____

Courses . . . Priority: _____

Schedule . . . Hours available per week: _____

Enjoy your online learning adventures!

Part 7

What Are They Talking About?

In these appendixes you will discover some important details, technical and otherwise. Appendix A deals with course management systems. Appendix B contains a glossary that gives definitions of key words. Appendix C discusses privacy and the loss of it online. In Appendix D you will learn where to find any other facts you need using links to resources and providers.

Appendix A: How Do They Do That?

What turns a professor at a four-walled college into an online teaching whiz in less time than you can say "class dismissed"? Services called *course management systems.*

An astonishingly short time ago, the most sophisticated "distance learning" was by video. Hard as it is to believe, also, not that long ago, computers could only be used by people with computer language and programming skills. The Internet itself was a hopeless jungle for most of us until not so many years ago, when the Web created pathways through it—and even then, only those with Hypertext Markup Language (HTML) skills could post messages on it. So learning via computer is only as recent as a few years ago, when a few schools put together computerized programs featuring their own teachers and links. Already, however, the boom is too big for that kind of simplicity. So how do providers respond to the need for more courses in more technologically advanced formats?

Course management systems (CMSs) developed quickly to meet the needs of teachers like the one quoted here:

> I am thoroughly enjoying developing my first online course with this service. The initial training and materials allow us to move forward quite quickly in the development process. With the user-friendly format, I am both challenged and inspired to do more with my classes.

CMSs work with faculty to convert courses for online delivery or provide online supplements for on-campus courses. In the following text are descriptions of some of them and how their services work to get education from the teacher to you. These and others are also good resources for testing out firsthand what distance learning is like and who provides it. (See the links at the end of this chapter and in Appendix D for more information.)

eCollege.com provides technology and services that enable colleges and universities to create virtual campuses through software products consisting of online courses and course supplements, as well as services including design, development, management, and complete hosting services. This CMS, like others, also provides ongoing support for administration, faculty, and students and can create an online "campus" that includes admissions, registration, bookstore, library, academic advising, career counseling, student union, and financial aid services. The company also promises to help educators incorporate the Internet into their systems or to provide a Web-based supplement to their in-classroom courses. eCollege.com offers online tools to help teachers step by step to post and update the syllabus, build an online calendar, and use e-mail for delivering lectures, testing, grading, and interacting with students. This service, like most of the others that are widely used (for example, Eduprise), is totally Web based and requires only a simple modem connection.

Another type of provider is represented by services like Prometheus, which offers more actual course content to its users. WebCT is among the services that provides "perforated" courses—material not designed and posted by a teacher, but created by "content providers"—as well as quizzes, activities, discussion guidelines, and other materials that teachers can simply select for use. These providers do offer support services for teachers, but they are more like texts or audiovisual materials than course creation architecture. These services also provide links to Web resources that teachers can use to supplement in-class activity.

A CMS (or a for-profit online university itself) may also connect with textbook publishers to provide not only structure but content. Many of the leading textbook publishers are linking up in this way. For instance, McGraw-Hill has a partnership with WebCT to enable McGraw-Hill content to be delivered to students who are enrolled through this Internet-based learning service.

The Wellspring is another type of Web based online distance learning resource. The Wellspring offers support through threaded discussions concerning teaching tips and instructional best practices. As well as courses, it provides online materials and articles.

Blue Web'n.com is an example of another kind of service—a searchable database of over 1000 Internet learning sites categorized by subject area, audience, and type (lessons, activities, projects, resources, references, and tools). Sites are presented through a tool that allows for the creation of a variety of classroom activities, which a professor simply has to select to produce material for any given class.

One of the largest course management providers (and actually the oldest, founded way back in 1997) is Blackboard, which was developed in collaboration with faculty members of Cornell University and provides a free online course Web service to help teachers and students with different levels of expertise create courses and class activities as well as share Web materials. The CMS provides the structure and also offers training as well as hosting services for colleges, universities, training programs, and grade schools.

Individual teachers can hook up with these services to create online courses, or schools or entire systems can sign on with a service—or point their teachers to one or various course management systems. Some educational institutions do provide their own services and support to help faculty members go online. Ohio State University (OSU), for instance, provides a campus resource that can help faculty develop distance education and course support Web pages. In-house services can meet special campus needs. For instance, OSU helps its faculty make Web pages accessible to all students, with guidelines for designing Web pages for the visually disabled in order to meet university and federal accessibility rules. Developers take faculty members step by step from evaluation through going live. The State University of New York (SUNY) maintains a large virtual education system through which it directs its faculty or departments to any of a variety of services.

At the end of this appendix is a list of links to various course management services. Exploring them can give you added insights into how the virtual education system works, and can also offer hands-on experience in participating in a distance course.

Step by step

Whatever service or system is used, a series of steps is recommended to develop and run an online course. Getting a distance course up and running requires some specialized skills, including:

- *Knowledge of Hypertext Markup Language (HTML) for putting items onto the Web.*

- *Knowledge of instructional design—a specialized educational system that is even more specialized for online learning. It includes not only the goals of teaching, but special needs of distance learners and special challenges of interaction with remote learners, effective visual graphics, and distance evaluation procedures.*

- *Training for instructors and administrators—distance learning instructors must be trained in the use of equipment and must develop instructional strategies and capabilities that ensure effective learning. Administrators need to understand the special needs of distance programs and how to support them and their instructors in new environments.*

- *Common Gateway Interface (CGI) coding to manipulate material gathered from Web sites. Especially since a large portion of these skills and information changes rapidly, most organizations choose to use a service or a specialized unit at their own institutions.*

- *Expertise in choosing equipment not only for performance, but also for compatibility and interoperability with industry standards, and the ability to upgrade and maintain equipment as technology continues to evolve.*

A CMS, of course, already has all that expertise. Whether to hire a service or rely on in-house abilities is one of the first issues to be decided in the place where most activities begin in academia—meetings. Here is an example of a typical procedure.

The first step toward high-tech education takes place in a series of low-tech, face-to-face conferences held to establish goals, survey resources, and make plans. Does distance learning fit with the overall needs and goals of the institution? Which systems will fit best?

An important matter to determine is whether a given course or program is actually suitable for online or Web-based presentation—not all courses are. At these stages, samples and hands-on presentations of possibilities from CMS providers can help guide the discussion.

Other decisions to be made involve what the online aspects will include. The possibilities:

- *Instruction itself—when and if it can be done more effectively than the face-to-face variety (simply putting lectures or notes online is not appropriate, for instance).*

- *Conferencing capabilities on the Internet or on campus through intranets, or simply class discussions, reports, and dramatizations.*

- *Access to source documents—providing links to original documents and other resource materials to allow students (and teachers) to move around as widely as possible throughout the net and campus resource.*

- *Chat sites to allow for distance conversations and joint study.*

In addition, do you want a secure server, accessible only to those who have paid and have passwords, or an open one available to anyone? Will you enable payment via the Web? Registration? Is this a project the entire school or department is going to undertake, or will individual teachers be allowed to devise their own distance courses? Will the people who develop the course be the same ones who teach and administer it? Where will the support—both fiscal and practical—come from? Who will promote and administer the course? Once a staff has decided on the overall structure of its learning web, it can determine whether to proceed on its own or sign on with a course management service.

What kinds of support services can you provide online? Promotion and registration, academic advising, distribution of course materials, access to library resources, office hours with instructors, feedback on assignments, and on-site learning facilitators are all possibilities. Which will you provide, and how? These are all issues that need careful thought before any "magic keys" are punched.

This is the point at which a service can come in particularly handy: helping faculty convert a course from in person to online in style, for example. In-house staff can also expect a service to help decide the best methods of Web-based delivery, systems for payment to the instructor, means of developing and connecting support and resource materials, and hookups with research and computer services on campus.

While services have great experience in getting courses online, they are no more magic than the computer itself: they are only as good as the material they work with. Teachers who have done this work say it's hard and complex—but it's up to the teachers and staff to keep track of the services. They need to be kept on time, for one thing, in order to be up and running when college marketing services have promised—and they need to be checked to ensure that the quality, content, and feel of the product are appropriate. The service has its own system and courseware, and is being paid to use it, but it's up to the school to keep track.

Common components of a Web course

Though details vary from school to school, here's what needs to be included on a learning site:

- *Static components include information that remains the same throughout the life of a course, such as:*

    ★ *Instructor's introduction—perhaps with a link to an individual site*

    ★ *Course description*

    ★ *Course prerequisites*

    ★ *Textbooks and other reading lists—with a link to the campus bookstore*

- ★ *Communications details: how students can reach teacher and each other; addresses, listserv, etc.*

- ★ *Course guidelines: syllabus, calendar of assignment dead-lines, rules of interaction, grading guidelines*

- • *Dynamic aspects of a Web site may change often or be expanded or updated regularly:*

  - ★ *Bulletin board*

  - ★ *Assignments list*

  - ★ *Communications systems*

  These allow interactivity in the course and include elements like:

  - ★ *Closed listservs, using e-mail addresses of class members*

  - ★ *Web forums, where people can interact and participate asynchronously*

  - ★ *Interactive real-time two-way audio or video, using spe-cially installed software to access high bandwidths for synchronous interaction*

  - ★ *Grade listings at a secure site*

  - ★ *Class notes site, where lecture notes and other ongoing items are regularly posted and archived*

- • *Many sites may also include:*

  - ★ *Audio clips*

  - ★ *Animations*

  - ★ *Video clips*

  - ★ *Self-correcting quizzes*

  - ★ *Case studies files*

  - ★ *Links to research resources*

  - ★ *Web database sites*

  - ★ *Web tutoring sessions—asynchronous or interactive*

Course management systems take teachers and administrators step by step (usually online) through the process of achieving these elements on their Web sites. You can get firsthand experience of how that happens by going to demos on the CMS Web sites listed in the following text.

Links to distance education service providers

The following links are useful for getting detailed information on how the providers work. You will also find links to other providers and resources for exploring distance learning on your own.

www.blackboard.com

www.eduprise.com

www.ed2go.com

www.quickplace.com

www.virtualu.com

www.ecollege.com

www.firstclass.com

www.prometheus.com

www.webcourse.com

www.e-education.com

www.intralearn.com

www.webct.com

www.wellspring.isinj.com

www.learn2.com

www.hungryminds.com

Appendix B: Glossary

No, you don't have to understand what all the words in this section mean in order to get what you need from online or other distance learning. These definitions are included here for clarification of some of the material in the book—and to give you an edge when you're asking questions about technologically delivered courses or deciphering instructions from your distance professors. You may be surprised at how simple are the meanings and sources of some of the more arcane-sounding phrases! The definitions here were collected from a variety of sources, including:

- *EdWeb*

- *CTCNet*

- *Catalyst Information Glossary from the University of Washington*

- *Distance Education Glossary from the University of Texas*

- *Federal Standards Telecommunications Glossary developed by the National Telecommunications and Information Administration (NTIA) of the U.S. Department of Commerce*

- *Glossary of Selected Distance Learning Terms and Phrases from the Public Health Training Network*

- *Glossary of Telecommunications Terms compiled by the Western Cooperative for Educational Telecommunications*

- *Glossary developed by the Lucent Corporation*

- *Teach Wisconsin Glossary from the University of Wisconsin extension program*

They comprise a traveler's phrasebook for your journeys into the foreign land of cyberspace. In addition, the more student-friendly individual education Web sites have their own glossaries, covering site-specific terms as well as these more general terms.

Access provider: a company that provides customers with Internet access connection by linking the customer's modem to the Internet via a regular telephone line.

ADSL (Asymmetric Digital Subscriber Line): a data communication medium that carries information on telephone lines at greater rates than audio transmission; *asymmetric* refers to the fact that downloading occurs faster than uploading, making browsing more efficient.

ALN (asynchronous learning network): a network of people linked for "anytime-anywhere" learning, using the Web and other remote learning resources, without the requirement to be online at the same time.

Analog: referring to electronic transmissions, a signal that is received in the same form in which it is transmitted, rather than having to be converted, as from electronic to auditory and back.

Analog modem: an older, slow form of modem that communicates over regular telephone lines by converting computer (digital) data into sound. At the receiving end, the data is then converted back to digital form.

Anonymous File Transfer Protocol (FTP): a system for retrieving documents, files, and programs from computers on the Internet that provides public access.

Applet: a small Java program that adds animation and interactivity to a Web site when it is downloaded.

ARPANet (Advanced Research Projects Agency Network): the forerunner of the Internet, developed by the Department of Defense in the late 1960s.

ASCII (American Standard Code for Information Interchange): a system that uses numbers to represent text, enabling different computers and programs to display the text in a uniform way.

Asynchronous: communication in which interaction between parties takes place at different times.

Attachment: a file, such as text or a spreadsheet, connected to an e-mail message in such a way that the recipient, using compatible software, can open or download it.

Audioconferencing: voice-only connection between more than two sites using standard telephone lines.

Audiographics: a live Internet combination of voice communications, computer networking, and graphics transmission using low-bandwidth telecommunications channels to link groups of users on a local area network (LAN), Internet, or low-bandwidth dial-up connection, making fully integrated, multiway audio conferencing accessible to all users.

Backbone: any large channel or communications path that connects multiple networks or users.

Band: a range of frequencies within defined upper and lower limits.

Bandwidth: the information-carrying capacity of a communication channel, measured in bits per second. The higher and wider the bandwidth, the faster the signal transmission.

Baud: a measure of the speed of data transmission, or the number thousand bits transmitted per second.

BBS (bulletin board system): like a real bulletin board, this virtual board is a place to post and read messages left by others via computer. Most BBSs charge a fee. The Internet's Usenet News BBS is free, though connecting costs a phone charge.

Binary: the number system that uses two digits, 1 and 0—known as *bits*—to produce all computer data.

Bit: the smallest unit of computer data, represented by 1 or 0.

Bitmap: a graphic image, like those on Web pages, formed by a pattern of dots or pixels. Some bitmap formats are Graphics Interchange Format (GIF), Joint Photographic Experts Group (JPEG), and Tagged Image File Format (TIFF).

Bookmark: an electronic method of saving a Web page's location for future access by a browser.

bps (bits per second): the speed at which data is transmitted over a channel; also known as *throughput*. Modem speeds are measured in bps, but referred to as *baud*.

Broadband: signals in the very fast ranges, used for personal communications services (PCSs) such as digital cellular phones and wireless Internet access.

Browser: software used to read electronic documents over the World Wide Web.

Byte: a combination of eight bits of data that represents a single character. A kilobyte is 1000 bytes, and a megabyte is 1 million bytes or 1000 kilobytes.

Cache: a temporary storage area to keep data available on a computer, making it easily accessible by Web browser software.

CAI (Computer-Assisted Instruction): a teaching process that uses a computer to assist students in gaining mastery over a specific skill.

CD-ROM (compact disc—read-only memory): a compact disc containing computer data such as programs, reference sources, or course materials for use in a CD-ROM drive.

Channel: any medium through which information can be transmitted; the smallest subdivision of a circuit.

Chat: online instant communication in an Internet area known as the Internet Relay Chat (IRC). Users participate by typing messages that appear on each other's computer screens.

Chat room (or chat channel): a virtual space created by computer software where participants in online electronic education can hold discussions, talking to each other by typing in messages on their computers that appear immediately on each participant's screen. Chat rooms are usually devoted to one particular topic.

Client: a software program (or the computer using the program) used to contact and obtain data from a server program located on another computer.

Coaxial cable (or cable wire): a standard copper transmission cable made up of an inner and an outer wire; used for older-style transmissions.

Compress: to shrink a file to save space and speed up transfers.

Computer conference: an asynchronous discussion group organized around a topic of discussion from its start to finish: each participant reads and comments over a period of time.

Cookie: a data file stored on the user's computer that allows Web site operators and advertisers to record the trail of sites that a person visits on the Web. Software is available to alert the user to the insertion of cookies, whose use is in the process of being regulated.

CPU (central processing unit): the unit of a computer where data processing takes place.

Cross-platform: software that works on any platform or hardware (e.g., PC or Macintosh). The Internet is cross-platform; proprietary software (like WordPerfect) is not.

Cyberspace: a term for virtual reality coined by novelist William Gibson. It now refers to the whole range of computers, networks, people, and information connected via the Internet.

Decode: to transfer the form of a file back from ASCII after encoding and transfer.

Dedicated line: a type of account available from an Internet service provider that connects the customer to the Internet 24 hours a day.

Dial-up account: an agreement with an Internet service provider to connect a customer to the Internet when the modem dials the provider's number.

Digital: made up of numbers, or digits. On a computer, the digits are binary—only 1s or 0s. Also describes any technology that converts or transmits information signals by breaking them into binary digits.

Digital modem: a modem that communicates computer data directly without having to convert it as an analog modem does; requires an Integrated Services Digital Network (ISDN) line and is faster than an analog modem. It uses a special digital phone.

Disk cache: a temporary storage area on a computer to keep data available. For instance, Web browser software keeps a certain number of Web pages available for revisiting.

Distance education: teaching and/or learning by way of telecommunications, or the process of providing instruction when students and instructors are separated by physical distance.

Domain name: a unique label for an Internet site.

Download: to bring files, programs, or any form of data onto your computer from another computer via the Internet.

DSL (digital subscriber line): a type of data communication technology used to deliver and receive information on current telephone lines at a much greater speed than phone service.

DVI (Digital Video Interactive): a format for recording digital video onto compact discs.

e: electronic anything; delivered online.

e-education: electronic education that uses online media for delivery.

e-mail (electronic mail): computer messages sent via the Internet or another computer network from one e-mail address to another.

e-mail address: electronic locator for e-mail delivery: a unique identifying name followed by the @ symbol and then the name of the host organization, which could be a business (.com), organization (.org), university (.edu), governmental entity (.gov), or or Internet service provider (.net).

Emoticons: faces made using keyboard symbols to be viewed sideways to add life to electronic communications.

Encode: to convert data to a special format for easier transfer between computers or systems.

Encryption: scrambling of data transmitted via the Internet, to ensure that only the recipient can decode and read it.

Ethernet: a system for linking computers over a local area network.

Extension: a three-character code at the end of a file name (after a dot) that identifies its type.

FAQs (frequently asked questions): information files provided by many Web sites to reduce the need for repetition of information.

Fax (facsimile): a system used to transmit visual images via standard telephone lines.

Fiber-optic cable: glass fiber that is used for laser transmission of video, audio, and/or data. Digital patterns of light pulses on fiber-optic channels are far faster than signals sent on copper cables.

Filters: a means to sort and categorize incoming e-mail. Junk or other unwanted messages can be screened out; messages can be sorted into files and folders.

Firewall: a computer security system placed between a local network and the Internet to prevent threats to or intrusions into internal systems.

Flame: an insulting or assaultive comment included in an Internet discussion, most often in newsgroups. Flames can expand into *flame wars*.

Frames: Web page layout style in which different content appears on separate areas of the page, allowing an index to remain stationary.

Freeware: software available for downloading from Internet sites without cost.

FTP (File Transfer Protocol): a system for moving files from a distant computer to a local computer using a network like the Internet.

Fully interactive video: two sites connected by audio and video as if they were not separated.

Gateway: a computer connecting two systems or networks, translating data to make it usable by both systems. America Online is a gateway between its users and the Inernet, though it is not directly on the Internet.

GIF (Graphics Interchange Format): a graphics file format used to place photographs and illustrations, animated or still, on Internet Web pages.

Gigabit: 1 billion bits of data.

Gopher: an Internet protocol that uses software to allow a user to navigate the Internet via a series of menus; designed to make File Transfer Protocol (FTP) simpler to use.

Hertz: a unit of frequency used to measure the electromagnetic waves by which sound, light, and energy are transmitted.

Hit: a term describing the numbers of clicks made to access a World Wide Web page. Not an accurate measure of those who actually use a page, because some browsers must click in several times to call a page up, and there's no indication of how long a user spends at a given page.

Home page: a document with an address (URL) on the World Wide Web, maintained by a person or organization, that contains information as well as pointers to other pieces of information.

Host: a single- or multiuser computer that can send and receive data over the Internet, making files or other resources accessible to other computers.

Hotlist: a list of URLs of Web sites stored by a browser to allow ease of retrieval; similar to a bookmark list.

HTML (Hypertext Markup Language): a system of codes used to create Web pages and access documents over the World Wide Web. Without HTML codes, a document would be unreadable by a Web browser.

HTTP (Hypertext Transfer Protocol): the protocol used to signify an Internet site, it occupies the initial place in all Web addresses.

Hybrid course: an educational program that combines various technologies for course delivery.

Hypertext: a document marked up with HTML to allow a user to click on selected words or icons within it to connect ("link") to further information.

Information Superhighway: nickname for what is officially known as the National Information Infrastructure (NII)—the interconnected global networks of communication and information services, including the Internet.

Interactive media: media that enable two-way interaction or exchange of information.

Interface: a connection between two pieces of hardware or software, or between a user and an application. Also, the appearance of a screen displaying a program—the collection of bars, buttons, colors, and shapes that assist in navigating and operating the program.

Internet: a global network of interconnected computer networks linked through a system called Internet Protocol (IP). Nicknamed the Net.

Internet discussion groups: also known as newsgroups, these are collections of individuals who post information and discussions via e-mail on subjects of mutual interest.

Intranet: an internal network for a company, school, or organization that uses the technology of the Internet rather than the complicated software of local area networks (LANs).

IP (Internet Protocol): the international standard for addressing and shipping data on the Internet.

IP address: a unique identification number consisting of four sets of numbers separated by dots. Every computer on the Internet has an IP address.

IRC (Internet Relay Chat): a section of the Internet where users can communicate with others by typing messages that appear on the monitors of other users as soon as they are sent. Also, the online group discussion itself; abbreviated as *chat.*

ISDN (Integrated Services Digital Network): a telecommunications service that sends digital signals—voice, video, and data—on several channels at once rapidly over telephone lines. It requires special hardware and software at both ends. ISDN eliminates the conversion and reconversion of data necessary in analog systems, making World Wide Web (WWW) access and File Transfer Protocol (FTP) transfers much more rapid.

ISP (Internet service provider): a company that provides a connection from a computer modem to the Internet using a regular telephone line.

ITFS (Instructional Television Fixed Service): microwave-based, high-frequency television used in educational program delivery.

IVC (interactive visual communication): two-way auditory and visual communication that gives users the ability to see the sites and people to which they are connected.

Javascript: a computer language used for the World Wide Web (WWW) that allows for adding interactivity to Web pages.

JPEG (Joint Photographic Experts Group): a type of graphics format for Web pages that provides generally better quality than Graphics Interchange Format (GIF) images, but consists of more data and so takes longer to load.

Keyword: a word or phrase sought by a search engine. Refers both to the word the user of the search engine types in and to the word listed by a Web site developer in an area of the Hypertext Markup Language (HTML) coding for a Web page called a *metatag.* The search engine software compares the two and provides a list of matches.

Kilobyte: 1000 bytes.

LAN (Local Area Network): a group of computers that are locally connected on a network.

Leased line (dedicated line): a phone line that is connected 24/7, primarily used for Internet activity.

Link (hotlink): Web text or pictures coded with Hypertext Markup Language (HTML) on a Web page, which, when clicked, allows a view of a different Web page on the same computer or a computer anywhere else in the world.

Listserv: an e-mail program or electronic mailing list that allows the distribution of messages to many individuals in one mailing and allows multiple computer users to connect to a single system for communication or discussion. Listserv groups can number in the millions, or may be small groups of people involved in, say, class discussions.

Login: the name of an account used to access a computer system, such as that of an Internet service provider (ISP). Usually used in conjunction with a personal secret password for limited-access sites. Also used as a verb, "to log in."

Lurk: to observe or read a Usenet newsgroup or other listserv without making oneself known. Announcement of one's presence is called *delurking*.

Lynx: a text-based World Wide Web browser, easier to read and accessible by older computers because it does not use graphics.

Mailing list: a list of users who will receive copies of information on a particular topic that is distributed periodically by e-mail. Mail server software, such as Listserv, receives contributions and distributes them to all subscribers.

Markup: text or codes added to a document to formulate a document's layout or to create links to other documents or information servers. Hypertext Markup Language (HTML) is a common form of markup.

MCU (Multi-point control unit): a computerized switching system that allows multipoint videoconferencing.

Megabit: 1 million bits of data.

Megabyte: a measurement of data—1 million bytes or 1000 kilobytes. Most commonly used to measure a working memory area of a computer.

Microwaves: electromagnetic waves that travel in straight lines and are used to transmit data to and from satellites and for short distances.

MIDI (Musical Instrument Digital Interface): a protocol for data exchange between music synthesizers and computers.

MIME (Multipurpose Internet Mail Extensions): a protocol that enables e-mail programs to carry various types of data.

Mirror site: a File Transfer Protocol (FTP) site that contains an exact copy of the files at another site; developed so that increased numbers of people can access files of popular sites.

MMDS (Multichannel Multipoint Distribution Service): a form of wireless cable service that transmits signals at high frequencies. Sometimes referred to as *wireless cable.*

Modem: short for *modulator/demodulator*—a hardware component that uses a telephone line to connect a computer to other computers by converting digital signals to analog signals for transmission along analog lines.

Moderated list: a Usenet newsgroup or mailing list where communications first go to an individual who serves as moderator and approves all items before they are distributed to the group or list.

MOO (multi-user object-oriented environment): a computer environment, similar to chat rooms, where groups such as students and faculty members come together at the same time (as opposed to e-mail and listservs, which are asynchronous) to discuss common issues. MOOs incorporate pictures; multi-user domains (MUDs) use only text.

MPEG (Motion Picture Experts Group): a protocol for compressing sound and movie files into a format for downloading or streaming over the Internet.

MUD (multi-user domain): a computer environment, similar to chat rooms, where groups such as students and faculty members come together at the same time (as opposed to e-mail and listservs, which are asynchronous) to discuss common issues. MUDs use only text; multi-user object-oriented environments (MOOs) incorporate pictures.

Multimedia: the use of more than one medium in transmitting information; in electronic communication, refers to the use of any combination of text, full-color images and graphics, video, animation, and sound; also, any document that uses multiple forms of communications media, such as text, audio, or video.

Multiplexing: an engineering technique that allows multiple signals to occupy the same amount of bandwidth by breaking signals into components or by superimposing several signals.

Nesting: the placing of documents within other documents, allowing a user to access material in a nonlinear fashion; a primary factor in the development of hypertext.

Netiquette: a set of generally accepted but informal guidelines for considerate conversation and behavior on e-mails and the Internet in general.

Network: a series of points connected by communication channels in different locations. Any collective of computers that can communicate and exchange data among themselves.

Newsgroup: the name given to an individual discussion group on Usenet.

Online: active and prepared for operation. Originally a military term, it now implies being connected to a computer network.

Online course: an educational program whose primary delivery source is the Internet. The course site on the Web is self-contained in that the student does not meet in person with other learners or the instructor. Communication is asynchronous, occurring through e-mail, listservs, multi-user object-oriented environments (MOOs), threaded discussions, and chat rooms.

Online service: a company that maintains a network of information, forums, and other services including Internet access, which charge a fee for participation. Among the major online services are America Online, CompuServe, and the Microsoft Network.

Open platform: a computer and network design concept within which all users of the Internet can access, create, and publish information as well as understand each other's information.

Operating system: a computer program used to provide basic services like files, screen information, and mouse use. Microsoft Windows and Apple MacOS are the most common operating systems for personal computers.

Origination site: the location from which a teleconference is sent.

Packet: a bundle of data of any size transmitted over a network as a way of improving communications efficiency.

Password: a series of letters and/or numbers used in conjunction with a user name to provide security while accessing a site or joining a class.

PCSs (personal communication services): the range of radio communication services for personal use, including wireless faxes, paging systems, digital cellular phones, etc.

PIN (personal identification number), or PID (process identifier): a personal identifier used as part of security on entering sites.

Plug-in: a program that adds extra functions to a Web browser. Audio and video, as well as Internet telephone, often require plug-ins, which can be downloaded from the Internet and installed on the user's computer.

Point-to-multipoint: transmission between multiple locations using a bridge.

Point-to-point: transmission between two locations.

POP (Post Office Protocol): an older protocol that enables an e-mail program to retrieve messages from a server.

Post: to send an e-mail to a listserv, bulletin board, or Internet discussion group.

PPP (Point-to-Point Protocol): a software package that provides a direct connection to the Internet over a telephone line.

Protocol: a formal set of standards, rules, formats, or systems that assures uniformity between computers and applications, as for exchanging data.

RAM (random access memory): allows a computer to keep information stored for instantaneous access, as opposed to retrieving it from a hard drive, which takes more time. Information in RAM is lost when you turn off the computer or lose power.

Ring: a local area network that connects a group of computers one after another until they form a ring.

Router: a relay that connects a local area network with other networks.

Satellite TV: video and audio signals relayed to a special receiver via a communication device that orbits around the earth.

Search engine: a Web site that hosts an indexed database of many of the Web sites in the world, to make searching them possible. The search engine is programmed to match words the user types in.

Server: a computer or program that allows other computers to access information on it, and functions on a network to receive and connect incoming information traffic.

Shareware: software that may be tried for free, then bought for a small payment if the user keeps the program.

SLIP (Serial Line Internet Protocol): a system that allows connection to the Internet directly over a high-speed modem.

Snail mail: nickname for regular paper mail from the U.S. Postal Service.

Spam: unwanted commercial e-mail, mass-mailed like paper junk mail. Can be filtered out.

Spectrum: the full range of electromagnetic frequencies used for all forms of transmission.

Surfing: as in *surfing the Web;* to move from one Web site or page to another Web site.

Synchronous: electronic interaction between participants simultaneously, in real time, as in chat rooms.

TCP (Transmission Control Protocol): a system that ensures that a computer's packets of data are shipped and received over a network in the right order. When used with Internet Protocol (IP), it is known as TCP/IP.

Telecommunications: the science of information transport using wire, radio, optical, or electromagnetic channels to transmit and receive signals for voice or data communications by electrical means.

Telecommuting: working at home by connecting to one's office (or classroom) through a computer network.

Teleconferencing: two-way electronic communication between two or more groups in separate locations via audio, video, and/or computer systems.

Telnet: a terminal emulation protocol for connecting to another computer elsewhere over the Internet.

Transponder: a satellite transmitter and receiver that receives and amplifies a signal for retransmission to an earth station.

Uplink: the communication link from an earth station to a satellite.

URL (Uniform Resource Locator): the address used to view a Web site; listed either as http:// or www.

Usenet: a network of thousands of Internet newsgroups—online discussion groups that can be accessed through a server connected to Usenet.

User name: ID by which a computer identifies a user sending e-mail or connecting to a remote site or computer.

Video teleconference: a distance learning medium in which students and faculty meet at the same time and can see and talk to each other using video cameras, microphones, and the Internet or telephone lines to connect between the sites. The distance between sites can be anything from less than a mile to the other side of the world.

WAN (wide area network): a network that covers a large region, such as a county or a state.

Wavelength: the length of one complete electromagnetic wave.

Web-based instruction: distance education whose primary delivery source is the Internet. The course site, found on the Web, contains detailed information about the course. It is self-contained in that the student does not meet in person with other learners or the instructor. Communication occurs through e-mail, listservs, multi-user object-oriented environments (MOOs), threaded discussions, and chat rooms. Most assignments and tests are completed and submitted online. However, for some courses students are required to take exams at a testing site.

Web browser: a software program that runs on your computer to connect it with the Internet and display information from Web sites. Microsoft Explorer and Netscape Communicator are examples.

Web site: a set of files on a computer on the Internet that has information that can be viewed with a Web browser.

WWW (World Wide Web): a graphical hypertext Internet navigational tool allowing access to sites, files, and home pages created by individuals, businesses, and other organizations. Also called the Web.

Appendix C: A Note About Privacy

Privacy on the Internet is a controversial issue, and it is not simply a matter of intellectual interest once you decide to sign on with an online education program. Privacy guidelines and government regulations may (or may not) be effectively in place, but it's up to you to initiate whatever protective measures you feel are appropriate for yourself. There are several factors to consider. One is the matter of personal disclosures that you may make during the course of your online classes, as noted earlier in the book. The psychology and atmosphere of the seemingly anonymous Internet seem to encourage premature intimacy, so it's especially important to remember that the Net is not really anonymous (your ID is accessible) and it's not intimate (anything you say can be forwarded around the universe). This may be okay with you—but you do need to be aware of it. When you get involved in a wider range of newsgroups or listservs, be a bit on your guard about how much personal information you reveal to strangers.

Another issue to think about is that, in order to sign on with an education provider—whether a university or a noncredit learning site—you need to provide personal and financial information. Rules limit how that information can be used, but it is accessible, even if by illegitimate means, so caution is wise. You should also be aware that education is increasingly being used as a come-on to get people into a commercial site—so what you think of as an educational project may actually be an excuse to get marketing data about you.

Cookies, those Web site–placed electronic slivers that lodge in your computer, will track you (for commercial purposes) wherever you go in your educational journeys. Thus, even if the educational provider doesn't directly impinge on your privacy, your increased use of the Web for research and the like leaves you vulnerable to a variety of cookies. You can set your software preferences to alert you to the prospect of cookie placement, with the option of allowing the cookie at sites where either you can't be admitted without it, or, perhaps, you want it. You will be astonished at how many times the cookie alarm will sound! Some people like the idea of all that attention being paid to them—and that's fine. But if you start getting a lot more junk mail both online and in your mailbox, you'll know you've been pegged! A more ominous kind of privacy probe is done by systems that actually try to break into your computer. When these probes work, they can conceivably be used to spread viruses or worse; but there's software available to alert you to that as well.

Finally, if you have your own Web site or participate in a college's Web site—or let your name be included in a college's student directory—remember that this area of the college site is public and accessible by anyone, so don't be surprised if you begin to get e-mail from new sources.

You needn't feel you're paranoid in any concern you have about matters of privacy. The *Chronicle of Higher Education* recently reported that "A notable 92 percent of online households agree or agree strongly with the statement, 'I don't trust companies to keep personal information about me confidential, no matter what they promise.' " A June 2000 article in the same publication also described the types of data retrieved and stored electronically by educational institutes for their on-campus students as well as online participants. This trend is so striking that it's raising serious practical and ethical questions, especially because "when it comes to protecting privacy rights . . . most colleges are behind the curve."

These days, just as your education is increasingly in your own hands, so is your privacy protection. You'll find further discussion of this issue at some of the general and academic sites listed in Appendix D.

Appendix D: Data Update

Why won't you find pages listing distance learning providers in this book? Because there are other sources available (which go out of date almost immediately). Instead, the following lists of sites and sources lead you to what you really need: resources to get up-to-the-second information about distance learning and its providers. Each—including some sites that do keep updated lists of providers—offers information about one or more aspects of distance learning, as well as links or connections to other general and specific sources of information and help that were useful when this book was written. Each of these sites offers free access—you needn't be a member or pay a fee to get the information or the links.

If you need more and newer information, you can search for yourself: enter keywords like "distance learning," "distance education," or "online learning" (using quotes or underscores) into the search commands of any leading search engine (Yahoo!, Netscape, Excite, etc.), and you'll find what's going on today in the virtual classroom. On the home pages of some of the search engines you'll even find a section to click for going directly to education links. Since this new world of learning changes so fast, you'll want to go to those links as well as the resources included here, which cover the following topics:

- *Resources for information about distance education and its providers*

- *Sources for some specifics on distance learning*

- *Links to examples of student-friendly distance learning sites and newsgroups*

- *Resources for information on education planning and adult education*

- *Resources for information about financial aid and extra credit*

- *Links to lists of providers and courses*

- *Training connections*

Resources for information about distance education and its providers

The Distance Learning Resource Network (DLRN)
A project of the U.S. Department of Education to disseminate distance learning information
www.dlrn.edu

Department of Education Home Page
A Wide network of links
http://nces.ed.gov/

The Distance Education and Training Council (DETC)
Informational resources on technology-based learning for both students and teachers
www.detc.org

The Distance Education Clearinghouse
From the University of Wisconsin Extension, providing information about distance education and its delivery
www.uwex.edu

The United States Distance Learning Association
P.O. Box 5129
San Ramon, CA 94583
Phone: 1-800-275-5162 or 510-606-5160
Fax: 510-606-9410
e-mail: charles@usdla.org

University Continuing Education Association
One Dupont Circle NW, Suite 615
Washington, DC 20036-1168

Phone: 202-659-3130
Fax: 202-785-0374
e-mail: postmaster@nucea.edu
www.nucea.edu

Pennsylvania State University
An instructional resource server at an electronic library of digitized
material available to distance education faculty and students,
accessible by a wider audience and including lists of and links to
courses taught with/through the Internet, lists of distance education sites, research sites in distance education, and video education sources.
www.outreach.psu.edu/users/atb/main.htm

AskERIC
ERIC is the Educational Resources Information Center, a federally
funded national information system that provides information on
all aspects of education to teachers, students, administrators,
researchers, and others.
http://ericir.syr.edu/

The Comprehensive Distance Education List of Resources
Links to distance education Web sites compiled by Illinois On-Line
Network at the University of Illinois.
http://illinois.online.uillinois.edu

AT&T Center for Excellence in Distance Learning
Research and reports related to distance learning
www.CEDL.com

The Teletraining Institute
A practical laboratory where teachers, corporate trainers, government
instructors, and others can learn and explore skills and methods.
www.teletrain.com

www.distance-educator.com
Well organized and regularly updated offerings for educators in distance learning.

EDUCAUSE
An international nonprofit association dedicated to transforming
higher education through information technologies; many of its
services are aimed at the information technology professional.

The Web site is useful for any educator or student seeking a better understanding of technology.
www.educause.org

International Centre for Distance Learning (ICDL)
A worldwide information clearinghouse for distance education
icdl@open.ac.uk

Annenberg/CPB Project
Support and information for colleges, schools, and community organizations on using telecommunications technologies to improve learning, as well as course resources for "free agent" learners
www.learner.org

www.searchedu.com
A searchable database of over 20 million international university and education pages indexed and categorized

http://www.uidaho.edu/evo/distglan.html
Online series of papers, reports, and explanations about all aspects of distance learning

http://galaxy.einet.net/galaxy/social-sciences/education.html
A great list and links for education sites related to all aspects of education

Sources for some specifics on distance learning

Course management services (CMSs) like the following are intended to help teachers and schools put together learning packages for their students. For teachers or trainers who sign on, they serve as free guides through the steps to create virtual classes—including registration, discussion, and testing, which are then hosted on the company's servers. Their sites are accessible by anyone and are excellent resources for information on how distance learning works, lists of schools and courses available online, and opportunities for hands-on demonstrations of online learning. Some originated as purely commercial ventures and have teachers on board to help; others were generated from colleges or groups of teachers, who then widened their reach by becoming commercial. Each is worth a look to learn more about the new education firsthand.

eCollege.com
www.ecollege.com

Blackboard
www.blackboard.com

WebCT
http://about.webct.com

Eduprise
www.eduprise.com

The Wellspring
A collaborative project from Instructional Systems Inc. and members of the Teachers College, a Columbia University community devoted to the needs of distance educators using the World Wide Web to deliver post secondary courses to their students.
http://wellspring.isinj.com

www.thenode.com
A collection of papers and interviews describing practitioners' experiences using integrated learning packages (CMSs) for the development and delivery of online courses.

Links to examples of student-friendly distance learning sites and newsgroups

Listservs

To access these, e-mail the site and type in "subscribe" as the message and on the subject line.

alt.education.distance
Usenet forum featuring discussion by students, instructors, and experts about distance learning at the collegiate level.

alt.education.university.vision2020
Usenet forum featuring discussion about education with a focus on distance and online learning.

DEOS-L-Request@PSUVM.PSU.EDU
Type in this message: "Subscribe DEOS-L."

Distance learning listservs

ASAT-EVA: AG-SAT Distance Education Evaluation Group
CONTED: *The International Journal of Continuing Education Practice*
CREAD: Latin American and Caribbean Electronic Distance Education Forum
CREAD-D: CREAD Workshop on Distance Education Quality Control
DED-L: distance education
DEOS-L: The Distance Education Online Symposium
DEOSNEWS: The Distance Education Online Symposium
HMEDRSCH: Home Education Research Discussion List
WVUPFF-L: Adult Education/Distance Learning Discussion Group

Resources for information on education planning and adult education

ACT, Inc. Information for Life's Transitions
2201 North Dodge Street
P.O. Box 168
Iowa City, IA 52243-0168
Phone: 319-337-1000
Fax: 319-339-3021
www.act.edu

American College Advisory Service (ACAS)
4455 Connecticut Avenue NW
Washington, DC 20008
Phone: 202-237-2500
Fax: 202-237-2900
e-mail: advising@acas.com

American Council on Education
Center for Adult Learning and Educational Credentials
One Dupont Circle NW, Suite 250
Washington, DC 20036-1193
Fax: 202-775-8578
www.ace.nche.edu

College Credit Recommendation Service
Phone: 202-939-9433
e-mail: mailto:credit@ace.nche.edu
Credit by Examination Program
Phone: 202-939-9434
e-mail: creditbyexam@ace.nche.edu

Council for Adult and Experiential Learning (CAEL)
243 South Wabash Avenue, Suite 800
Chicago, IL 60604
Phone: 312-922-5909
Fax: 312-922-1769
www.cael.org

Center for Career, Education and Life Planning
New York University School of Continuing and Professional Studies
145 Fourth Avenue
New York, NY 10003
Phone: 212-998-7060
e-mail: advice.scps@nyu.edu

Resources for information about financial aid and extra credit

Federal Student Aid Information Center
phone: 1-800-4-FED-AID (1-800-433-3243)

Department of Education
Office of Postsecondary Education
1990 K Street NW
Washington, DC 20006
Questions or Comments on Student Financial Aid

College Level Examination Program (CLEP)
P.O. Box 6600
Princeton, NJ 08541
Phone: 609-951-6106 or 1-800-257-9558
Fax: 609-734-5410
e-mail: clep@ets.org

Links to financial resource information

www.embark.com
www.finaid.org

Books

Earn College Credit for What You Know
by Lois Lamdin
Available from CAEL, 243 S. Wabash Avenue, Suite 800, Chicago,
    IL, 60604, phone: 312-922-1769
How to get college credit for work and life experience

The Distance Learning Funding Sourcebook
by Arlene Krebs
Available from Kendall/Hunt Publishing Company, 4050 Westmark
    Drive, Dubuque, Iowa, 52004-1840, phone: 800-228-0810
www.technogrants.com

Bear's Guide to Finding Money for College
by John Bear, PhD and Mariah Bear, MA.
TenSpeed Press, 1998
Information on financing most kinds of education

Links to lists of providers and courses

America's Learning Xchange
A prototype of a new service to help people find out who offers
    training or education.
www.alx.gov

Asynchronous Learning Network
Focuses on helping students locate opportunities from a pool of
    existing programs
www.netlearning.org

International Telecomputing Consortium (ITC)
A national nonprofit organization that represents postsecondary
    educational institutions that are involved in distance learning. An
    affiliated Council of American Association of Community Col-

leges, ITC represents over 500 educational institutions from across the United States and Canada.
www.itc.org

Telecampus Online Courses Database
Lists 9000 Internet courses
www.telecampus.edu

The Internet University
An indexing service that lists articles, courses, and study; more than 2,440 courses listed
www.caso.com

MindQuest Cybercourses and Distance Education Resources
Virtual distance learning, including courses and consulting services
www.mindquest.com

For lists of accredited distance courses

Council for Higher Education Accreditation (CHEA)
One Dupont Circle NW, Suite 510
Washington, DC 20036-1110
Phone: 202-955-6126
Fax: 202-955-6129
e-mail: mailto:chea@chea.org

International Association for Continuing Education and Training
1200 19th Street NW, Suite 300
Washington, DC 20036
Phone: 202-857-1122
Fax: 202-223-4579
e-mail: iacet@dc.sba.com

United States Department of Education
Office of Postsecondary Education
Accreditation and State Liaison Division
ROB-3, 7th and D Streets SW
Washington, DC 20202
Phone: 202-708-7417
Fax: 202-708-9469

Training connections

American Society of Training Directors (ASTD)
Offers services to members but also many services to nonmembers,
including an online library and lists offering links to 400,000
training program sites of online training providers. Other information available here includes costs of training and consultants,
lists of other related professional groups, and reading lists categorized by specific topic.
1640 King Street, Box 1443
Alexandria, VA, 22313-2043
Phone: 703-683-8100
Fax: 703-683-8103
www.astd.org/virtual_community

@brint.com: The BizTech Network
One of the best known for knowledge management networking and
links. The bulk of @brint.com's content lies in three divisions:
e-business, general business, and knowledge management.
www.brint.com

Other training sites of general interest, where you can also find demos

www.learningtechnologies.com

www.presenters university.com

www.gilgordon.com

www.trainingassociates.com

www.brandonhall.com

The Masie Center
Provides a great deal of information on both training activities and
vendors
www.masie.com

Learnativity
Points to organizations, Web sites, publications, tools, books, and
discussion lists related to career development. You can also find

links to training industry statistics, trends, salaries, Web tools, articles, and certification.
www.learnativity.com

Of the hundreds of thousands of online training providers, the following are some that provide generalized offerings, which can serve as examples of what you're likely to find when you seek training at a distance:

DPEC, Inc.
Offers several hundred Web-based training courses that require no downloading because they are delivered interactively to your browser.
www.dpec.com

GeoLearning Inc.
A leading provider of Internet and intranet-based training, computer-based training, and performance support systems for all organizations on a variety of subjects in several formats including diskette, CD-ROM, network versions, Internet/intranet delivery, video, and print.
www.geolearning.com

NIIT NetVarsity
Offers extensive courses in Internet technologies, Web publishing, and open client servers. Students have access to a virtual library.
www.netvarsity.com

Virtual Classrooms of America
Provides interactive training for a wide range of personal computer (PC) desktop applications both on CD-ROM and through its On Line University.
www.virtualclassrooms.com

Digital University
Offers over 40 courses as well as links to additional courses and to regulatory, legal, and operational information sites; designed for financial institutions
www.digitaluniversity.com

Edge Interactive
Delivers comprehensive training solutions for technical systems installation and maintenance, business applications, and end user skills
www.edge.com

SMGnet
Provides online learning, simulation, and custom solutions in financial management, marketing, project management, sales, and leadership

Cytation Corporation
Develops and licenses online learning systems and services to businesses and organizations offering packages of training designed for special needs
www.cytation.com

eMind.com
An online destination for continuing education. Courses are offered to professionals in industries such as accounting, securities, and insurance.
www.emind.com

Futuremedia
A joint venture with British Telecom, this CMS is a net-based learning and knowledge management service that offers the means to create, publish, distribute, manage, assess, and track all online learning materials.
www.futuremedia.com

Knowledge Communication, Inc.
Creates simulation-based training applications for professional development in which students learn by doing, by exploring, and by applying their skills
www.knowledgecommunication.com

AthenaOnline.com
Contains 45- to 60-minute management and career development programs. Also includes free management articles and streaming video lectures.

Index

About the Author

Sara Dulaney Gilbert is the author of more than 25 books on education and self-help, including *The Career Training Sourcebook*, also available from McGraw-Hill, and *How to Do Your Best on Tests*. Her articles have been published in national magazines. Ms. Gilbert holds an MA from the New York University School of Education, and has worked as an administrator in higher education institutions for nearly two decades.